WORDS,
MORE WORDS

and

Ways To Use Them

Editorial Development: Karen Doyle

Manufacturing/Production: James W. Gibbons

Illustrations: Marcy Ramsey

Cover Design: Marshall Henrichs

Printed in the United States of America.

ISBN: 0-201-53961-6

1 2 3 4 5 6 7 8 9 10-AL-96 95 94 93

CONTENTS

How to Use this Book

WORDS, MORE WORDS AND WAYS TO USE THEM is designed to help you improve your vocabulary and reading skills. This workbook is divided into 5 units, and each unit has two to seven chapters. Each chapter covers topics from normal, everyday life with words associated with the topic.

Each chapter is divided into three sections: **Words to Know, Word Practice,** and **Reading Practice.**

Words to Know
The Words to Know vocabulary list may contain some words you already know. You should review these words, but concentrate on the words that are new to you. You might find it useful to use this book with a dictionary.

Word Practice
Each word in the vocabulary list is used in one of the activities in the Word Practice section. These activities will teach you how to quickly recognize the words from their spelling patterns, how to categorize them, and how to define and use them.

Reading Practice
The Reading Practice section has three types of questions similar to those on tests like the TOEFL and the TOEIC: Error Recognition, Paragraph Comprehension, and Conversation Comprehension.

The underlined words in the Error Recognition section may contain errors of the following grammatical types:

Word Families	Two-Word Verbs
Prepositions	Articles
Conjunctions	Pronouns
Adverbs of Frequency	Subject-Verb Agreement
Causative Verbs	Modal Auxiliaries
Conditional Sentences	Adjective Comparisons
Verb Tense	Gerunds and Infinitives

Each unit ends with some task-based activities that use the vocabulary introduced in the chapters: **Start Talking, Put It In Writing,** and **Act It Out.**

Start Talking

Start Talking has a variety of communicative games that will help you and your classmates develop your listening and speaking skills and use the vocabulary you learned in the preceding chapters.

Put It in Writing

The writing section will help you develop the communicative skills used when writing. The activities here focus your attention on a writing task that requires you to use the vocabulary in the chapter.

Act It Out

This section allows you and your classmates to practice your dramatic skills. You will continue to use the chapter's vocabulary while acting out a mini-drama.

You do not need to start with Chapter One. You may start anywhere in the workbook and study only those chapters where you need to improve your vocabulary.

You should write your answers directly in the book and compare your answer with the answers given in the Answer Key. The Answer Key is in the back of the book.

AT HOME

How many words from this unit can you identify. Write the words on the lines. Draw lines from the picture to the words.

curtains

toaster

1 BODY

WORDS TO KNOW

ankle	face	knee	shoulder
arm	finger	leg	stomach
back	fist	lip	thigh
beard	foot/feet	moustache	throat
cheek	forehead	mouth	thumb
chest	hair	muscle	toe
chin	hand	nail	tongue
ear	head	neck	tooth
elbow	heart	nose	waist
eye	hip	palm	wrist

WORD PRACTICE

1. Label these parts of the body.

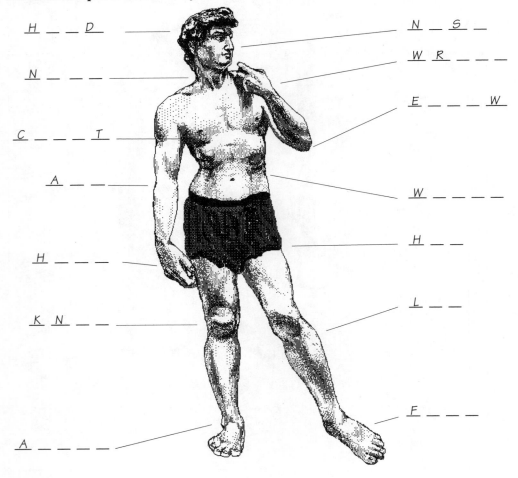

H _ _ D _ _ _ _ _

N _ _ _ _ _ _

C _ _ _ T _ _ _

A _ _ _ _

H _ _ _ _ _

K N _ _ _ _ _

A _ _ _ _ _

N _ S _

W R _ _ _ _

E _ _ _ W

W _ _ _ _

H _ _

L _ _

F _ _ _

2. Idiom Practice: Complete the sentences.

1. He's at the H E A D of his class. = *He's the best.*

2. Don't try to E __ __ __ __ your way in. = *Don't push yourself in.*

3. I've got them in the P __ __ __ of my H __ __ __ . = *I'm in control.*

4. He has a L __ __ up on this. = *He has the advantage.*

5. I have two left F __ __ __ . = *I'm very clumsy.*

6. Don't M __ __ __ __ __ in. = *Don't try to be a part of this.*

7. Keep your L __ __ __ sealed. = *Don't talk.*

8. She gave me the cold S __ __ __ __ __ __ __ . = *She ignored me.*

9. I can't S __ __ __ __ __ __ his opinion. = *I don't like his opinion.*

10. He's all T __ __ __ __ __ . = *He's very clumsy.*

11. He has a big M __ __ __ __ . = *He can't keep a secret.*

12. She has a sharp T __ __ __ __ __ . = *She is unkind.*

13. Keep your E __ __ __ peeled. = *Look out for something.*

14. Turn the other C __ __ __ __ . = *Forgive someone.*

15. I know the city like the back of my H __ __ __ . = *I know it very well.*

16. He has a H __ __ __ __ of gold. = *He is kind.*

17. He wears his H __ __ __ __ on his sleeve. = *Everyone knows when he's in love.*

18. This job is a pain in the N __ __ __ . = *This job bothers me.*

19. We don't see E __ __ to E __ __ . = *We don't agree.*

20. He turned his B __ __ __ on us. = *He ignored us.*

3. Complete these sentences.

1. Hair covers the top of the H E A D .

2. A moustache is under the N __ __ __ .

3. A beard covers the C __ __ __ .

4. Both toes and fingers have N __ __ L S .

5. The F __ __ __ H __ __ D is between the eyebrows and the hairline.

4. Cross out the word that does NOT belong.

1. lip   mouth   ~~toe~~
2. chin   thigh   beard
3. fist   hand   neck
4. nose   ankle   moustache
5. hip   eye   shoulder
6. thumb   finger   wrist
7. tongue   forehead   tooth
8. stomach waist   toe
9. ankle   foot   head
10. arm   nail   elbow

READING PRACTICE

1. Which underlined word is incorrect? Circle the letter.

> **GRAMMAR TO KNOW:**
> gerunds   articles
> subject-verb agreement   verb tense

1. When Joseph pounded <u>his</u> fist, he <u>hurts</u> <u>his</u> finger.
                   A   Ⓑ C

2. When I <u>closed</u> <u>my</u> eyes, I cannot <u>see</u>.
        A   B   C

3. The heart <u>is</u> a muscle that <u>pump</u> blood <u>throughout</u> the body.
          A   B   C

4. Because you <u>cut</u> your foot, you may <u>find</u> <u>to walk</u> difficult.
          A   B   C

5. Stephanie's forehead <u>and</u> cheeks are so hot she thinks she <u>had</u> <u>a</u> fever.
               A   B C

6. When Rocky was <u>punched</u> <u>in</u> <u>a</u> chin, he got a toothache.
           A   B C

7. <u>My</u> nose and mouth <u>is</u> <u>too</u> large for my face.
   A   B C

8. <u>Eaten</u> too many sweets <u>may</u> <u>cause</u> a stomach ache.
   A   B   C

9. My father <u>has</u> a thick beard, <u>so</u> you cannot <u>saw</u> his chin.
         A   B   C

10. Pam has <u>a</u> broken wrist so she <u>can't</u> play <u>the</u> tennis for two months.
       A   B   C

2. Read the following conversation and answer the questions.

Man:	My right arm hurts. I wonder if my heart is OK.
Woman:	You should see a doctor, and, in the meantime, rest.
Man:	My doctor can't see me until tomorrow.

1. What is the problem?
   (A) The doctor is resting.
   (B) The man is too busy.
   (C) His right arm hurts.

2. What does the woman want the man to do?
   (A) See a doctor
   (B) Get out of bed
   (C) Wait until tomorrow

3. What should he do in the meantime?
   (A) Exercise
   (B) Rest
   (C) Study medicine

4. When is the doctor available?
   (A) Presently
   (B) This evening
   (C) Tomorrow

3. Read the following paragraph and answer the questions.

Clothes should be comfortable as well as attractive. Shoes must be wide enough for the toes; pants must be long enough in the legs and wide enough at the waist. Jackets must not be tight across the chest, and sleeves should not be too short for the arms.

1. Pants must not be too narrow at the
   (A) chest
   (B) waist
   (C) shoulder

2. Shoes must not be too narrow for the
   (A) fingers
   (B) toes
   (C) ears

3. Jackets must fit comfortably across the
   (A) palm
   (B) ankle
   (C) chest

4. Sometimes the sleeves may not fit the
   (A) arms
   (B) legs
   (C) feet

2 CLOTHES

WORDS TO KNOW

alter	glove	raincoat	sock
belt	handbag	running shoes	suit
blouse	hat	scarf	sweater
boots	jacket	shirt	take off
briefcase	lapel	shoelace	tennis shoes
button	overcoat	shoes	tie
coat	pants	skirt	trousers
collar	pocket	slacks	try on
cuff	put away	sleeve	T-shirt
dress	put on	sneakers	umbrella

WORD PRACTICE

1. Complete the following sentences.

1. I put on my _S_ _O_ _C_ _K_ _S_ before I put on my shoes.

2. If it is raining, I wear a _R_ _ _ _ _C_ _ _ _ and carry

   an _U_ _ _B_ _ _ _ _ _A_ .

3. I broke a _S_ _ _ _ _ _A_ _ _ when I was tying my shoes.

4. I use a _B_ _ _ _ to hold up my pants.

5. If the weather is cool, I will wear a _S_ _W_ _ _ _ _ _ .

6. The shirt _C_ _ _ _ _ _R_ is too tight around my neck.

7. A _B_ _ _ _ _ _N_ is missing from my shirt cuff.

8. The color of her _S_ _K_ _ _ _ matches her _H_ _ _ _D_ _ _ _G_ .

9. It's windy so I'll wear a _J_ _ _ _K_ _ _ .

10. The tailor who added _C_ _ _ _F_ _ to my pants charges for alterations.

2. Draw a line between similar items of clothing.

blouse ——————————— overcoat

raincoat ———————————— slacks

tennis shoes ———————shirt

pants ———————————— sneakers

3. Label the clothes.

1. _GLASSES_
2. _____
3. _____
4. _____
5. _____

6. _____
7. _____
8. _____
9. _____
10. _____

4. Which of the following are referred to "in pairs?" Write them below.

pants	handbag	belt	socks
T-shirt	shoes	trousers	boots
slacks	gloves	jacket	hat

1. A pair of _____PANTS_____   5. A pair of _____

2. A pair of _____   6. A pair of _____

3. A pair of _____   7. A pair of _____

4. A pair of _____

5. Write the word under the appropriate category.

	WORN ABOVE THE WAIST	WORN BELOW THE WAIST
tie	_TIE_	_____
shirt	_____	_____
boots	_____	_BOOTS_
shorts	_____	_____
running shoes	_____	_____
shoe laces	_____	_____
tennis shoes	_____	_____
T-shirt	_____	_____
sweater	_____	_____
jacket	_____	_____

6. Complete the following sentences.

    1. In the morning when I get dressed, I put _O_ _N_ my shirt before I

       __ __ __ on my pants.

    2. In the evening before I go to bed, I take __ __ __ my shoes before I

       __ __ __ __ off my socks.

    3. When my shirts come back from the laundry, I put them _A_ __ __ __ .

7. Fill in the blanks.

    1. On my feet I wear _S_ _H_ _O_ _E_ _S_ .

    2. On my head, I wear a _H_ __ __ .

    3. Around my neck I wear a _S_ __ __ __ __ or a _T_ __ __ .

READING PRACTICE

1. Which underlined word is incorrect? Circle the letter.

> **GRAMMAR TO KNOW:**
> articles   infinitives
> subject-verb agreement   verb tense

    1. <u>My</u> new jacket needs <u>being</u> altered <u>because</u> the sleeves are too long.
       A   Ⓑ   C

    2. Suzanne <u>always</u> carries a purse <u>but</u> a briefcase when she <u>goes</u> to work.
             A   B   C

    3. Will you <u>got</u> my wallet? <u>It's</u> <u>in</u> my pants pocket.
             A   B C

    4. When wearing <u>a</u> suit, the right choice <u>of</u> a tie and shoes <u>are</u> essential.
                A   B   C

    5. Scott <u>wear</u> his boots <u>to</u> work every day <u>and</u> puts on his shoes in the office.
            A   B   C

    6. I <u>was</u> getting my raincoat <u>and</u> umbrella out <u>of</u> the closet now.
      A   B   C

    7. Bob <u>came</u> dressed casually, in tennis shoes, <u>a</u> T-shirt <u>also</u> running shorts.
        A   B   C

    8. Will you <u>try on</u> this sweater?   It <u>didn't</u> <u>fit</u> me anymore.
             A   B C

    9. These slacks <u>need</u> a belt <u>because</u> they <u>is</u> too big for you.
             A   B   C

    10. If you want <u>wearing</u> one <u>of</u> my skirts, or a blouse, you <u>may</u>.
            A   B   C

2. Read the following conversation and answer the questions.

> Customer: I would like this suit altered, please.
> Tailor: Please try it on for me.
> Customer: I want to have the sleeves shortened, and the lapels made narrower.
> Tailor: What about the pants? Do you want a cuff?
> Customer: No, I prefer pants without a cuff.

1. What does the customer want altered?
   (A) His suit
   (B) His shirt
   (C) His coat

2. What is wrong with the sleeves?
   (A) They're too short.
   (B) They're too long.
   (C) They don't match.

3. What does he want made narrower?
   (A) His sleeves
   (B) His cuffs
   (C) His lapels

4. How does he prefer his pants?
   (A) Tight around the waist
   (B) With a cuff
   (C) Without a cuff

3. Read the following passage and answer the questions.

> I am a very neat person. I keep my bedroom very neat, too. My bedroom closets are very organized. I hang all my shirts together. I hang all my pants together. I hang all my suits together. All of my shoes are arranged in rows on the floor. My ties and belts hang on the closet door. I keep my raincoat and my overcoat in the hall closet downstairs.

1. How would you describe this person?
   (A) Disorganized
   (B) Neat
   (C) Polite

2. Where does he put his shirts?
   (A) In the closet
   (B) In drawers
   (C) Across a chair

3. What does he hang on the closet door?
   (A) His pants
   (B) His suits
   (C) His ties

4. What does he keep in the hall closet?
   (A) His raincoat
   (B) His suits
   (C) His shirts

3 THE LIVING ROOM

WORDS TO KNOW

armchair	couch	lamp	shelf
ashtray	curtains	lamp shade	shelves
bookcase	cushion	mantel	sofa
carpet	drapes	mirror	stereo
ceiling	end table	painting	television
chair	fireplace	picture	wall
coffee table	floor	rug	woodwork

WORD PRACTICE

1. Write the words below for things found on the wall.

1. <u>M</u> <u>I</u> <u>R</u> <u>R</u> <u>O</u> <u>R</u>   4. <u>P</u> __ __ __ __ __ <u>E</u>

2. <u>W</u> __ __ <u>D</u> __ __ __ <u>K</u>   5. <u>S</u> __ __ __ __ __ <u>S</u>

3. <u>M</u> __ __ __ __ <u>L</u>   6. <u>P</u> __ __ __ __ __ __ <u>G</u>

2. The words for some things are often written in plural form. Write them here.

SINGULAR	PLURAL
1. curtain	_CURTAINS_____
2. shelf	_____
3. end table	_____
4. drape	_____
5. picture	_____
6. chair	_____

3. Write the appropriate preposition for each of the following sentences.

CHOICES: in, on, to, above, under

1. The cushions are _____ O N _____ the sofa.

2. The books are kept _____ the bookcase.

3. The end tables are next _____ the sofa.

4. The mantle is _____ the fireplace.

5. The carpet is _____ the furniture.

6. The carpet is _____ the floor.

4. Fill in the blanks.

Many living rooms have a _F_ _I_ _R_ _E_ _P_ _L_ _A_ _C_ _E_ . Above the fireplace is the _M_ __ __ __ __ _L_ , which is a kind of _S_ __ __ __ _F_ used to display special things. Above that is a space where there is often a large _M_ __ __ __ __ _R_ , or a special _P_ __ __ __ __ __ __ _G_ .

5. Look at the floor plan. Circle the correct preposition.

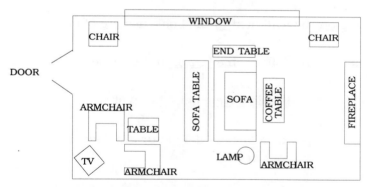

1. There is a chair ((on) / in) either side of the window.

2. There are chairs on both sides (of / to) the window.

3. The coffee table is (in front of / to the side of) the sofa.

4. The sofa table is (behind / over) the sofa.

5. The fireplace is (across from / next to) the door.

6. The TV is (at / in) the corner.

7. There is a small table (between / in front of) the armchairs.

8. There is a lamp (beside / behind) the armchair by the sofa.

9. The end table is (next to / in front of) the sofa.

10. The sofa is (around the corner from / in front of) the fireplace.

6. Draw a line between the nouns that make noun phrases. Write the noun phrase next to it.

NOUN	+	NOUN	NOUN PHRASE
1. lamp		tray	*LAMP SHADE*
2. wood		chair	
3. ash		shade	
4. arm		case	
5. book		place	
6. fire		work	

READING PRACTICE

1. Which underlined word is incorrect? Circle the letter.

> **GRAMMAR TO KNOW:**
> conjunctions   prepositions
> subject-verb agreement   verb tense

1. Every night, Stanley sits <u>above</u> the armchair <u>and</u> <u>watches</u> television.
                         (A)   B   C

2. The painting <u>on</u> the wall next <u>to</u> the bookcase <u>are</u> of our Aunt Martha.
           A   B   C

3. The soda fell <u>off</u> the coffee table <u>but</u> <u>onto</u> the carpet.
           A   B C

4. The lamp <u>on</u> the end table <u>have</u> <u>a</u> beige lamp shade.
           A   B C

5. If the contractor builds a low mantel <u>of</u> our fireplace, we can <u>put</u> a large
                            A   B
   mirror <u>above</u> it.
         C

6. The curtains <u>but</u> the cushions <u>on</u> the sofa are <u>made</u> of the same fabric.
           A   B   C

7. The woodwork <u>in</u> the <u>Edwards'</u> living room <u>match</u> the mantel.
           A   B   C

8. <u>Below</u> Emily's stereo <u>is</u> three shelves <u>of</u> records.
     A   B   C

9. The ceiling <u>in</u> our living room is very high, <u>so</u> the room <u>appeared</u> large.
           A   B   C

10. The drapes <u>on</u> our living room windows are thick, and <u>allowed</u> very little
           A   B
    light to come <u>into</u> the room.
            C

2. Read the following conversation and answer the questions.

Byron:	Do you want the mirror over the sofa or by the door?
Melinda:	Over the sofa is fine. What about the end table?
Byron:	Let's put it by the armchair.
Melinda:	That's perfect. The painting can go over the bookcase.
Byron:	And we can put the coffee table in front of the sofa. There! Finished!

1. Where does Melinda want the mirror to go?
   (A) Over the sofa
   (B) Outside
   (C) By the door

2. What are Byron and Melinda doing?
   (A) Sitting on the sofa
   (B) Arranging furniture
   (C) Selling antiques

3. Where will the painting be hung?
   (A) Above the sofa
   (B) Between the windows
   (C) Over the bookcase

4. Where will the coffee table go?
   (A) Next to the armchair
   (B) By the end table
   (C) In front of the sofa

3. Read the following paragraph and answer the questions.

Many families use their living rooms as a place for relaxation. It is a place to converse, watch TV, or play music on the stereo. Other families use their living rooms as a more formal place with elegant furniture. They keep the TV and stereo in a family room. They use the living room only when company comes to visit.

1. For many families the living room is a place for
   (A) exercising
   (B) relaxing
   (C) eating

2. Elegant furniture makes a living room
   (A) playful
   (B) rustic
   (C) formal

3. What would NOT fit in a formal living room?
   (A) A TV
   (B) Elegant furniture
   (C) Oil paintings

4. Formal living rooms are used primarily when
   (A) the dining room is too small
   (B) the stereo is broken
   (C) there is company

4 THE KITCHEN

WORDS TO KNOW

bottle	counter	knife	salt shaker
bowl	cup	napkin	saucer
broiler	cutlery	oven	sink
burner	dish	pan	spoon
cabinet	dishwasher	pepper shaker	stove
can	fork	placemat	table
chair	garbage can	plate	tablecloth
coffee maker	garbage disposal	pot	toaster
cook	glass	refrigerator	trash can

WORD PRACTICE

1. Write in the words for electrical appliances.

1. _D_ _I_ _S_ _H_ _W_ _A_ _S_ _H_ _E_ _R_

2. _T_ _ _ _ _ _T_ _ _R_

3. _R_ _ _ _ _ _ _ _ _ _ _T_ _ _R_

4. _C_ _ _ _ _ _E_   _ _ _ _R_

5. _G_ _ _ _ _ _ _ _D_ _ _ _ _ _ _L_.

2. Circle the words for items found on a table. (6 words)

oven	spoon	cup
(plate)	cabinet	cook
glass	salt shaker	napkin

3. Circle the correct word.

1. We can cook food in a ((pan) / dishwasher).
2. A (saucer / trash can) goes under a cup.
3. You can wash dishes in the (spoon / sink).
4. Most people use a (can /cabinet) to store dishes.
5. A (toaster / tablecloth) helps keep a table clean.
6. We throw (garbage / salt) away.
7. Put the cutlery on the (placemat / burner).
8. The cook mixed the ingredients in the (bowl / toaster).
9. Put the meat under the (broiler / oven) to cook.
10. Use one (cup / spoon) of water to make one cup of coffee.

4. Write the singular form.

SINGULAR	PLURAL		SINGULAR	PLURAL
1. _TABLECLOTH_	tablecloths	6. _____		dishes
2. _____	knives	7. _____		bottles
3. _____	glasses	8. _____		cabinets
4. _____	stoves	9. _____		placemats
5. _____	salt shakers	10. _____		napkins

5. Cross out the word that does NOT belong.

1. ~~road~~   tablecloth   placemat
2. plant   fork   knife
3. bottle   can   lamp
4. table   counter   ceiling
5. seat   glass   cup
6. stove   window   refrigerator

6. Write the word that completes the pair.

1. Cup and _S A U C E R_   3. Pots and _P _ _ S_
2. Knife and _F _ _ __   4. Salt and _P _ _ _ _ R_

7. Complete the question.

1. What is _C U T L E R Y_?

   Knives, forks and spoons.

2. What is a _C _ _ _ _ _   M _ _ _ __?

   An appliance that brews coffee.

3. What is a _G _ _ _ _ _ _   D _ _ _ _ _ _ L_?

   An appliance that grinds garbage.

4. What is an _O _ _ __?

   A place where meat is roasted or bread is baked.

5. What is a _T _ _ _ _ _ R_?

   An appliance that browns bread.

READING PRACTICE

1. Which underlined word is incorrect? Circle the letter.

> **GRAMMAR TO KNOW:**
> conjunctions   pronouns
> subject-verb agreement   articles

1. <u>To set</u> the table, we'll <u>need</u> plates, knives, forks, placemats <u>or</u> glasses.
   A   B   ©

2. Kevin <u>keeps</u> his pots <u>but</u> pans in the cabinet <u>below</u> the stove.
        A   B   C

3. We don't <u>has</u> a garbage disposal so we <u>throw</u> garbage <u>in</u> the garbage can.
          A   B   C

4. Little Amy's baby bottle and <u>she</u> dish <u>are</u> in <u>the</u> dishwasher.
                               A   B C

5. Will you please <u>pass</u> me the salt shaker <u>and</u> the bowl of <u>the</u> spaghetti?
             A   B   C

6. Angela's counter <u>have</u> many appliances <u>on</u> it: the coffee maker, the
                    A   B

   toaster, <u>and</u> the can opener.
          C

7. <u>Our</u> want coffee so we'll <u>need</u> cups, saucers, <u>and</u> spoons.
  A   B   C

8. If you want <u>to cook</u> dinner <u>in</u> the oven, turn <u>them</u> to 350 degrees.
           A   B   C

9. The food <u>from</u> last night's dinner that <u>were</u> not eaten <u>is</u> in the refrigerator.
         A   B   C

10. Do you want <u>to cook</u> the hamburgers <u>in</u> the oven <u>and</u> on the stove?
          A   B   C

EVERYDAY EXPRESSIONS WITH COOKING TERMS

1. Cooking with gas =
   Thinking/acting efficiently
2. Cooking on all four burners =
   To be very alert and active
3. Don't cry over spilled milk. =
   Don't have regrets.
4. Half-baked idea =
   Not a well thought-out plan
5. Look at the pot calling the kettle black. =
   The accuser is also guilty.
6. The kitchen cabinet =
   A small group of close friends and advisers

2. Read the following conversation and answer the questions.

Bill:	Shall I set the table?
Susan:	Yes. Use the placemats, not a tablecloth.
Bill:	Do you want paper or cloth napkins?
Susan:	Paper. And we won't need plates. This soup will be the whole meal. We'll only need bowls.
Bill:	OK. No forks or knives either. Just spoons, right?

1. What is Bill going to do?
   (A) Buy napkins
   (B) Make soup
   (C) Set the table

2. What will they use on the table?
   (A) A tablecloth
   (B) Placemats
   (C) Furniture polish

3. What kind of napkins will they use?
   (A) Paper
   (B) Cloth
   (C) Plastic

4. What cutlery will they use?
   (A) Knives
   (B) Forks
   (C) Spoons

3. Read the following paragraph and answer the questions.

> Modern kitchens are different from older kitchens in several ways. There are more appliances, of course. Usually the modern kitchen is larger. There is more counter space for food preparation. Modern kitchens are also full of light. There are many more windows than in older kitchens.

1. This paragraph compares modern and older
   (A) windows
   (B) counters
   (C) kitchens

2. Modern kitchens are not
   (A) different
   (B) dark
   (C) large

3. In a modern kitchen there is more space to prepare
   (A) light
   (B) food
   (C) appliances

4. Why does the modern kitchen have more light?
   (A) Brighter bulbs
   (B) More lamps
   (C) More windows

5 HOUSEWORK

WORDS TO KNOW

ammonia	detergent	mop	sponge
bleach	dry	paper towel	starch
broom	dust	polish	sweep
bucket	dustpan	rag	wash
clean	iron	rug shampoo	washing machine
cleanser	ironing board	scrub	water
cord	make the bed	soap	vacuum cleaner

WORD PRACTICE

1. Add *-ing* to the following verbs.

1. sweep   _S W E E P I N G_

2. dust   _____

3. wash   _____

4. clean   _____

5. polish   _____

6. iron   _____

7. dry   _____

> **Note these differences:**
>
> mop   mopping
>
> scrub   scrubbing

2. Use the *-ing* words from Exercise 1 to complete these sentences.

1. The woman is _S_ _W_ _E_ _E_ _P_ _I_ _N_ _G_ with a broom.

2. Many people do spring _C_ __ __ __ __ __ __ __ .

3. We use a _W_ __ __ __ __ __ __ machine to wash clothes.

4. She is _D_ __ __ __ __ __ __ tables with a rag.

5. _P_ __ __ __ __ __ __ __ __ wood makes it shine.

6. To press clothes, an _I_ __ __ __ __ __ __ board is necessary.

7. _S_ _C_ __ __ __ __ __ __ __ will remove heavy dirt.

8. You need to have a bucket full of soap and water and a mop when

    _M_ __ __ __ __ __ __ floors.

3. Draw a line between the words that are similar in meaning.

broom ———————————————— rag
sponge   clean
soap   mop
wash   vacuum
sweep   cleanser

4. Cross out the words that do NOT belong.

1. soap	~~iron~~	water
2. bucket	cleanser	cord
3. sweep	detergent	washing machine
4. mop	sponge	shower
5. polish	yard	floor

5. Write types of cleaning products.

1. W A T E R
2. C _ _ _ _ S _ R
3. R _ G S _ _ _ _ _ O
4. P _ _ _ _ H
5. D _ _ _ R _ _ _ T
6. A M _ _ _ _ A
7. B _ _ _ _ H
8. S _ _ P

6. Write the appropriate cleaning product below.

1. I add A M M O N I A to water when I clean the windows.

2. B _ _ _ _ _ H keeps white clothes looking white.

3. Ajax is a C _ _ _ _ _ S _ R that cleans sinks.

4. Put D _ _ _ _ _ _ _ _ T in the washing machine with the clothes.

5. Use very little wax P _ _ _ _ H on wood furniture.

6. There is a roll of P _ P _ _ _ _ _ _ _ _ S by the sink.

7. Plain W _ _ _ R is usually enough to clean.

8. Using a R _ _ S H _ _ _ _ _ will keep your rug clean.

CLEANING EXPRESSIONS

1. Spring cleaning =
   A thorough cleaning
2. Dishpan hands =
   Hands rough from doing dishes
3. Use a bit of elbow grease. =
   Work harder/ rub harder.
4. Sweep the dirt under the rug. =
   Hide a problem.
5. This place is a pig pen. =
   It's really dirty.

READING PRACTICE

1. Which underlined word is incorrect? Circle the letter.

> **GRAMMAR TO KNOW:**
> conjunctions   conditional sentences
> infinitives   subject-verb agreement

1. <u>Sweeping</u> a floor, you need <u>a</u> dustpan <u>and</u> a broom.
     Ⓐ   B   C

2. Some people <u>put</u> both bleach <u>or</u> detergent into the washing machine to
               A   B
   wash <u>their</u> clothes.
        C

3. If <u>a</u> vacuum cleaner <u>can't</u> clean your rug, <u>tried</u> using rug shampoo.
     A   B   C

4. My shirt <u>were</u> wrinkled, <u>so</u> I <u>ironed</u> it with starch.
          A   B C

5. Steve, who <u>hates</u> dirt, <u>scrub</u> his kitchen floor <u>every</u> Saturday.
          A   B   C

6. When the floor <u>gets</u> dirty, Beth <u>cleans</u> it with soap, hot water <u>also</u> a mop.
          A   B   C

7. The vacuum cleaner <u>would</u> not turn <u>on</u> if its cord is <u>broken</u>.
             A   B   C

8. <u>Pours</u> ammonia, water <u>and</u> cleanser <u>into</u> a bucket for tough cleaning jobs.
     A   B   C

9. <u>Every</u> morning <u>before</u> work, Alice <u>make</u> her bed.
     A   B   C

10. In order to <u>cleaning</u> the tub, <u>use</u> some cleanser <u>and</u> a sponge.
           A   B   C

2. Read the following conversation and answer the questions.

Mother:	Here are today's chores: First, vacuum the rug. Then, sweep the steps and wash the windows.
Child:	How do I sweep the steps?
Mother:	With the broom, of course. And wash them after you sweep them.
Child:	Where are the bucket and mop?
Mother:	In the closet. The sponges and ammonia are in there, too.
Child:	Ammonia? What for?
Mother:	For the windows. And don't forget to make your bed and wash the breakfast dishes.
Child:	What about washing the clothes?
Mother:	Good idea. Don't use too much bleach.

1. What does the mother want done first?
   - (A) Vacuum the rug
   - (B) Sweep the steps
   - (C) Wash the windows

2. What will the child use to sweep the steps?
   - (A) A broom
   - (B) The vacuum
   - (C) The mop

3. What is NOT in the closet?
   - (A) Sponges
   - (B) Ammonia
   - (C) Dishes

4. What is the ammonia for?
   - (A) Cleaning windows
   - (B) Washing clothes
   - (C) Drying clothes

3. Read the following paragraph and answer the questions.

> Today many married people share housework equally. A wife may cook, and a husband may clean the house. A wife may wash windows while a husband may scrub the floors. When a husband and wife each have jobs, housework is the responsibility of both.

1. People who share housework are often
   - (A) married
   - (B) single
   - (C) separated

2. Sometimes a woman cooks while her husband
   - (A) paints
   - (B) travels
   - (C) cleans

3. Why do husbands and wives both do housework?
   - (A) Both are divorced
   - (B) Both have jobs
   - (C) Both need money

4. Housework is a
   - (A) hobby
   - (B) responsibility
   - (C) challenge

6 | FOOD

WORDS TO KNOW

apple	cookie	meat	rice
bacon	corn	milk	rotten
beans	cracker	oil	salad
bread	cream	old	salt
butter	egg	onion	sandwich
cake	fish	orange	stale
carrot	flour	peach	stew
cereal	fresh	pear	sugar
cheese	grapes	pepper	tea
chicken	ice cream	pie	tomato
coffee	lettuce	potato	vinegar

WORD PRACTICE

1. Write the following kinds of foods.

DAIRY GOODS

1. _B U T T E R_
2. _E_ _ _ _S_
3. _C_ _ _ _ _ _E_
4. _M_ _ _ _K_
5. _C_ _ _ _ _M_

BAKED GOODS

1. _C R_ _ _ _ _ _ _S_
2. _C_ _ _ _E_
3. _C O_ _ _ _ _S_
4. _B_ _ _ _ _D_
5. _P_ _ _

2. Cross out the word that does NOT belong.

1. eggs   ~~plant~~   meat
2. cake   pie   fish
3. fresh   milk   stale
4. cook   drive   serve
5. animal   pear   apple

3. Draw a line between food products that are often used together.

eggs   butter
bread   vinegar
coffee   cake
salt   lettuce
ice cream   bacon
tomatoes   pepper
oil   cream

4. The words for some food products are usually used in the singular form. Write them here.

1. _S_ _A_ _L_ _T_
2. _F_ _ _ _ _H_
3. _C_ _ _ _ _N_
4. _R_ _ _ _E_
5. _L_ _ _ _ _ _ _E_

6. _S_ _ _ _ _R_
7. _C_ _H_ _ _ _ _E_
8. _B_ _ _ _ _N_
9. _M_ _ _ _K_
10. _P_ _ _ _ _ _R_

5. The words for some food products are often used in the plural form. Write them here.

SINGULAR	PLURAL		SINGULAR	PLURAL
1. egg	_EGGS_		4. bean	
2. potato			5. onion	
3. grape			6. cookie	

6. Write the ingredients to make the following dishes.

1. Make a cake

   _B_ _U_ _T_ _T_ _E_ _R_
   _E_ _ _ _ _S_
   _F_ _L_ _ _ _ _
   _M_ _ _ _K_
   _S_ _ _ _ _

2. Make a salad

   _L_ _ _ _ _ _ _E_
   _O_ _ _
   _V_ _ _ _ _ _ _
   _T_

3. Make a chicken sandwich

   _B_ _R_ _ _ _ _
   _B_ _ _ _ _ _R_
   _L_ _ _ _T_ _ _ _
   _C_ _H_ _ _ _ _ _
   _T_ _ _ _ _ _ _ _

4. Make a stew

   _M_ _ _ _T_
   _S_ _ _ _T_
   _P_ _ _ _P_ _ _
   _C_ _ _ _ _ _ _
   _O_ _N_ _ _ _ _

READING PRACTICE

1. Which underlined word is incorrect? Circle the letter.

> **GRAMMAR TO KNOW:**
> conjunctions   prepositions
> subject-verb agreement   verb tense

1. <u>When</u> we returned from vacation, we <u>find</u> stale bread <u>and</u> rotten, old
   A   Ⓑ   C

   lettuce in the refrigerator.

2. Mom's apple pie <u>are</u> the perfect afternoon <u>snack</u> or <u>dessert</u>.
                    A   B   C

3. Every Sunday, the Petersons <u>eat</u> bacon <u>and</u> eggs <u>of</u> breakfast.
                                A   B   C

4. If you are hungry, <u>eat</u> some <u>of</u> the pears, oranges <u>but</u> grapes in
                       A   B   C

   the fruit bowl.

5. Last night we <u>ate</u> fresh fish with corn <u>and</u> rice <u>in</u> dinner.
                 A   B   C

6. My favorite recipe <u>are</u> the one <u>with</u> chicken, beans, <u>and</u> cheese.
                       A   B   C

7. If you <u>would</u> like a cup of coffee, <u>took</u> some cream <u>and</u> sugar.
          A   B   C

8. I <u>making</u> simple salads <u>with</u> lettuce, tomatoes, oil <u>and</u> vinegar.
     A   B   C

9. <u>Stop</u> snacking on cookies <u>and</u> crackers. Dinner will be <u>at</u> one hour.
   A   B   C

10. David always <u>puts</u> salt <u>and</u> pepper <u>at</u> his meat before eating it.
                 A   B   C

FOOD EXPRESSIONS

1.   Food for thought =
     Something to think about

2.   He's the apple of her eye. =
     She is very fond of him.

3.   Bring home the bacon. =
     Earn a living

4.   He's no spring chicken. =
     He's not very young.

2. Read the following conversation and answer the questions.

John:	Are these eggs fresh?
Bill:	No, I bought them last week. The bread is a week old, too.
John:	No wonder it's stale.
Bill:	And this milk tastes sour.
John:	That milk is two weeks old. Like the lettuce.
Bill:	Everything in this refrigerator is rotten.

1. How does John describe the eggs?
    (A) Not fresh
    (B) Sweet
    (C) Expensive

2. What is stale?
    (A) The eggs
    (B) The milk
    (C) The bread

3. How does the milk taste?
    (A) Sweet
    (B) Sour
    (C) Creamy

4. What describes the food in the refrigerator?
    (A) Rotten
    (B) Fresh
    (C) Tasty

3. Read the following paragraph and answer the questions.

> The supermarket has special sections for different kinds of foods. Milk, cream, and cheese are kept in the Dairy Section. Chicken, fish, and meat are kept in the Meat Section. Canned fruits and vegetables are kept on shelves. Fresh fruits and vegetables are kept in the Produce Section. Baked goods like bread, pies, cakes, and cookies also have their own sections.

1. Where is cream kept?
    (A) With the coffee
    (B) In the Dairy Section
    (C) With the canned goods

2. What is NOT in the Meat Section?
    (A) Chicken
    (B) Fish
    (C) Fruits

3. Where are fresh vegetables found?
    (A) In the Produce Section
    (B) In the Bakery Section
    (C) On the canned goods shelves

4. What are breads, pies, and cakes?
    (A) Canned goods
    (B) Baked goods
    (C) Produce

7 MONEY

WORDS TO KNOW

bank	charge	money	quarter
billfold	check	nickel	receipt
bills	coin	pay	save
budget	credit card	payment	small change
cash	dime	penny	spend
cent	dollar	piggybank	tax
change	earn	purse	wallet

WORD PRACTICE

1. Draw a line between words with similar meanings.

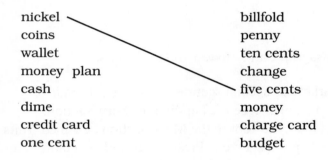

nickel	billfold
coins	penny
wallet	ten cents
money plan	change
cash	five cents
dime	money
credit card	charge card
one cent	budget

2. Write the Present Tense form (1st person singular) for the Past Tense verbs.

PRESENT PAST

1. _SPEND_____ spent

2. _____ charged

3. _____ paid

4. _____ earned

5. _____ saved

3. Cross out the word that does NOT belong.

1. dime   ~~bank~~   nickel   penny
2. purse   wallet   billfold   tax
3. forget   spend   save   earn
4. cash   credit card   check   meal
5. coins   bills   pen   money

4. Supply the words for types of coins.

    1. A <u>Q</u> <u>U</u> <u>A</u> <u>R</u> <u>T</u> <u>E</u> <u>R</u> and a <u>D</u> __ __ __ = 35 cents.

    2. Two <u>D</u> __ __ __ <u>S</u> and a <u>N</u> __ __ __ __ __ = 25 cents.

    3. Two <u>Q</u> __ __ __ __ __ __ <u>S</u> = 50 cents.

    4. Three <u>N</u> __ __ __ __ __ __ and five <u>D</u> __ __ __ <u>S</u> = 65 cents.

    5. Three <u>Q</u> __ __ __ __ __ __ __ and twenty-five <u>P</u> __ __ __ __ __ __ =

    one __ __ __ __ __ __ .

5. Complete the following sentences.

    1. It is necessary to have <u>C</u> <u>O</u> <u>I</u> <u>N</u> <u>S</u> for a parking meter.

    2. People usually write a <u>C</u> __ __ __ __ for large purchases.

    3. Always get a <u>R</u> __ __ __ __ __ __ as proof of purchase.

    4. Children often save their pennies in a <u>P</u> __ __ __ <u>Y</u> __ __ __ <u>K</u> .

    5. Most people pay <u>T</u> __ __ __ <u>S</u> to the government.

    6. You can pay for something later with a <u>C</u> __ __ __ __ __ <u>C</u> __ __ __ .

6. Complete the questions.

    1. What is a <u>R</u> <u>E</u> <u>C</u> <u>E</u> <u>I</u> <u>P</u> <u>T</u> ?

    A piece of paper with the cost of an item and its purchase date.

    2. What is a <u>C</u> __ __ __ __ __ <u>C</u> __ __ __ ?

    A small plastic card used instead of checks or money.

    3. What is a <u>B</u> __ __ __ __ __ <u>L</u> __ ?

    A pocket-sized case for carrying paper money.

    4. What is a <u>P</u> __ __ __ __ __ __ ?

    The amount of money paid or to be paid.

    5. What is a <u>B</u> __ __ __ __ __ ?

    An itemized summary of future

    income and expenses.

Reading Practice

1. Which underlined word is incorrect? Circle the letter.

> **GRAMMAR TO KNOW:**
> modal auxiliaries   articles
> subject-verb agreement   prepositions

1. Jason always <u>keep</u> all his bills neatly <u>tucked</u> into <u>a</u> billfold.
               Ⓐ   B   C

2. I <u>will</u> like to save <u>some</u> money to pay my <u>own</u> college tuition.
     A   B   C

3. I have <u>a</u> ten-dollar bill. <u>Do</u> you <u>has</u> any smaller change?
        A   B   C

4. If you have no cash, you <u>can</u> charge <u>this</u> dinner <u>of</u> your credit card.
                      A   B   C

5. Alison <u>keeps</u> all her pennies <u>on</u> <u>a</u> piggybank.
       A   B C

6. Mrs. Larson keeps <u>the</u> wallet <u>and</u> a checkbook <u>in</u> her purse.
                A   B   C

7. I <u>has</u> quarters, dimes, nickels, <u>and</u> pennies in <u>a</u> coinpurse.
     A   B   C

8. Jackie tries to stick <u>to</u> a budget, <u>but</u> she always spends more money than

   she <u>shall</u>.
     C

9. <u>A</u> change <u>from</u> my ten-dollar bill was <u>less</u> than 50 cents.
     A   B   C

10. At the end of <u>the</u> year, my taxes <u>amount</u> <u>of</u> thirty percent of my earnings.
                A   B   C

> **MONEY EXPRESSIONS**
> 1. A fool and his money are soon parted. =
>   Foolish people spend their money foolishly.
> 2. My money is burning a hole in my pocket. =
>   I can't wait to spend my money.
> 3. Pocket money =
>   Change for small purchases
> 4. Stretch your dollar. =
>   Make your dollar buy more.

2. Read the following conversation and answer the questions.

Anthony:	I'm taking the bus into town for food.
Kate:	Be sure to take plenty of coins. You need exact change to ride the bus now.
Anthony:	Can you change a five-dollar bill for me?
Kate:	Let's see. Here are three ones, and a lot of change, but it's less than five dollars.
Anthony:	That's okay. I'll take it. I need the change.

1. Where is Anthony going?
   (A) To the bank
   (B) Into town
   (C) To work

2. Why does Anthony need lots of change?
   (A) To ride the bus
   (B) To pay for groceries
   (C) To change buses

3. How much money does Kate have?
   (A) Exactly $5
   (B) Less than $5
   (C) More than $5

4. What did Kate do?
   (A) Take the bus
   (B) Give change to Anthony
   (C) Spend the $5

3. Read the following paragraph and answer the questions.

> People are using checks and credit cards for their daily purchases more and more. However, there are still times when only cash will do. Most vending machines will only accept cash. Parking meters only take change, and some only take quarters. Buses also require exact change.

1. What can checks and credit cards be used for?
   (A) Vending machines
   (B) Daily purchases
   (C) Buses

2. Only coins can be used for
   (A) Parking meters
   (B) Daily purchases
   (C) Bank deposits

3. What is required for parking meters?
   (A) Checks
   (B) Credit cards
   (C) Coins

4. What requires exact change?
   (A) Buses
   (B) Trains
   (C) Planes

UNIT ACTIVITIES

START TALKING

1. Creature Feature (Partners)

Create an unusual creature on a piece of paper. Describe it to your partner. Your partner will try to draw the creature from your description.

> *Example*   My creature has four legs, three eyes, and a long neck. It has two fingers and very short arms. It has no nose and no ears. Its mouth is very small.

Compare your drawing with your partner's.

2. I'm Hungry (Class Game)

Think of a favorite food (chicken sandwich, carrots, chocolate ice cream). Your classmates will ask questions to guess what the food is.

> *Example*

Student 1:	Can you drink it?
Student 6:	No.
Student 2:	Is it round?
Student 6:	No.
Student 3:	Is it a fruit?
Student 6:	Yes.
Student 4:	Can you eat it raw?
Student 6:	Yes.
Student 5:	Is it yellow?
Student 6:	Yes.
Student 5:	Is it a banana?
Student 6:	YES!

3. How Much? (Partners)

Plan a favorite meal. Write a shopping list for the meal. Give the list to your partner who (like a cashier) will put the price of each item and total it. You only have $10.00. What items will you be able to buy?

4. Make Yourself at Home (Class or Partners)

Think of each room in a house. Name one activity you like to do and one you hate to do in that room.

> *Example*
> Bathroom
> I hate to clean the bathtub.
> I like to brush my teeth.

PUT IT IN WRITING

1. Write a description of one of your classmates. The teacher will collect all the descriptions and read them aloud. The students will guess which student is being described.

2. Write a description of your favorite (or most disgusting) meal.

Variation:
Write how to prepare one of these meals.

3. You are getting ready for a party. Make a list of all the things you have to do. Which will you do first, second, third?

ACT IT OUT 1

Functions
Offering help
Asking for help
Expressing confusion
Expressing annoyance
Describing clothes by color

Characters
Roommate 1
Friend
Roommate 2

Setting
A friend is visiting a disorganized person. A roommate is in the next room looking for something.

Roommate 1:	(Frustrated) I need to clean this place. I can't find anything.
Friend:	(Concerned) What are you missing?
Roommate 1:	I'm missing my shirt, a sock, my left shoe, and my right glove.
Friend:	Where did you look?
Roommate 1:	(Exasperated) Everywhere in every room.
Friend:	Did you look behind the sofa?
Roommate 1:	(Discouraged) I looked behind, under, and all around the sofa.
Friend:	Did you look in the hall closet?
Roommate 1:	(Even more discouraged) I looked in the hall closet, the bathroom closet, and the bedroom closet.

Roommate 2:	What's the matter?
Roommate 1:	I can't find my shirt, a sock, my left shoe, or my right glove.
Roommate 2:	That's funny. I'm missing my jeans, a sock, my right shoe, and my left glove.
Friend:	What color was your shirt?
Roommate 2:	White.
Friend:	What color were your jeans?
Roommate 2:	Blue, of course.
Friend:	What color was your sock?
Roommate 2:	Red.
Roommate 1:	(Suspicious) Hey! So was mine.
Friend:	What color was your shoe?
Roommate 2:	Black.
Roommate 1:	(Getting angry) Hey! Mine, too.
Friend:	What color was your glove?
Roommate 2:	Brown.
Roommate 1.	(Exploding) That's it! You have MY glove!
Roommate 2:	(Defensive) And you have MY jeans, MY sock, and MY shoe.
Roommate 1:	You mean you have MY shirt, MY sock, and MY shoe.
Roommate 2:	(Embarrassed, but stupid) No wonder they don't fit.

ACT IT OUT 2

Do the skit again with different lost items.

Warm Up

Need
I can't find my _____.
             item

Where's my _____?
             item

Suggestion
Did you look _____?
                  location

Try the _____.
              location

ACROSS THE CITY

How many words from this unit can you identify. Write the words on the lines. Draw lines from the picture to the words.

8 | THE CITY

WORDS TO KNOW

alley	drive	museum	stadium
apartment house	entrance	newspaper stand	stop sign
boulevard	fire station	office building	store
building	freeway	opera house	street
bus stop	highway	parking lot	street light
city hall	hospital	parking meter	street sign
concert hall	hotel	phone booth	suburb
crosswalk	house	police station	subway
curb	lane	road	station
downtown	movie theater	sidewalk	traffic light

WORD PRACTICE

1. Circle the correct word.

1. This light turns green, red or yellow. It tells traffic when to stop or go.
   It is a ((traffic light)/ street light).

2. This light comes on at night. It helps people see when it's dark.
   It is a (traffic light / street light).

3. This sign is red. It is shaped like this: STOP Cars stop at this sign.
   It is a (stop sign / street sign).

4. This sign is usually green. It is shaped like this: ▬▬ It has the name of
   a street on it.
   It is a (stop sign / street sign).

5. I want to take an underground train.
   I should wait at a (bus stop / subway station).

6. I want to take the crosstown bus.
   I should wait at a (bus stop / subway station).

7. I want to make a phone call.
   I should go to a (newspaper stand / telephone booth).

8. I want to buy a newspaper.
   I should go to a (newspaper stand / telephone booth).

2. Write the words for types of buildings.

1. Workers work here:

   <u>O</u> <u>F</u> <u>F</u> <u>I</u> <u>C</u> <u>E</u> building

2. This is a city government building:

   <u>C</u> __ __ __   <u>H</u> __ __ __

3. A place to watch a movie:

   <u>M</u> __ __ __ __   __ __ __ __ __ __ __

4. Many people live here:

   <u>A</u> __ __ __ __ __ __ __ __   <u>H</u> __ __ __ __

5. A place to listen to a symphony:

   <u>C</u> <u>O</u> __ __ __ __ __   <u>H</u> __ __ __

6. A place to see exhibitions:

   <u>M</u> <u>U</u> __ __ __ __

7. A theater for opera:

   <u>O</u> <u>P</u> __ __ __   <u>H</u> __ __ __ __

8. Sick people get help here:

   <u>H</u> __ __ __ __ __ __ __

9. Travelers sleep here:

   <u>H</u> __ <u>T</u> __ __

3. Write the words for types of roads.

1. <u>S</u> <u>T</u> <u>R</u> <u>E</u> <u>E</u> <u>T</u>   5. <u>F</u> __ __ __ __ __ __

2. <u>R</u> __ __ __   6. <u>L</u> __ __ __

3. <u>H</u> __ __ __ __ __   7. <u>D</u> __ __ __ __

4. <u>A</u> __ __ __   8. <u>B</u> __ __ __ __ __ __ __ __

4. Complete the following paragraph.

Crossing the Street

     The pedestrians waited on the <u>S</u> __ __ __ <u>W</u> __ __ __ for the traffic light to change. When the sign across the street said "WALK," they stepped off the <u>C</u> __ __ __ and walked across the busy street in the <u>C</u> __ __ __ __ <u>W</u> __ __ __ .

5. Complete the following paragraph.

Parking
John drove into the city. He didn't have enough change for a
_P_ __ __ __ __ __ __ _M_ __ __ __ __ so he looked for a
_P_ __ __ __ __ __ __ _L_ __ __ , but they were all full. "Next time,
I'll take the bus," he thought.

READING PRACTICE

1. Which underlined word is incorrect? Circle the letter.

> **GRAMMAR TO KNOW:**
> conjunctions   gerunds
> prepositions   verb tense

1. Each morning she waits <u>at</u> the bus stop <u>in</u> the corner <u>for</u> the downtown

                  A   (B)   C

   express bus.

2. When the man <u>crossed</u> the street, he <u>did</u> not notice that the traffic light

                      A   B

   <u>has turned</u> green.

        C

3. Our office building <u>has</u> a store <u>but</u> a movie theater <u>on</u> the first two floors.

                 A   B   C

4. I do not <u>drive</u> to work.   <u>Park</u> <u>in</u> a parking lot is too expensive.

          A   B   C

5. <u>On</u> Saturday, I would <u>enjoy</u> <u>to go</u> to a symphony at the concert hall.

    A   B   C

6. <u>The</u> parking meter next <u>of</u> the telephone booths <u>is</u> out of order.

    A   B   C

7. When guests <u>come</u> to the city to <u>visit</u> me, they always <u>stayed</u> at a hotel.

             A   B   C

8. Traffic <u>at</u> the freeway this morning was <u>moving</u> <u>slowly</u>.

        A   B   C

9. <u>Got</u> into the right lane, turn <u>at</u> the next road <u>and</u> you'll see City Hall.

    A   B   C

10. The <u>riders</u> left <u>the</u> subway station <u>while</u> walked to the museum.

        A   B   C

2. Read the following paragraph and answer the questions.

> The Department of Streets and Highways announced today that a new highway connecting downtown and the suburban airport will be built. The 10-mile highway will be six lanes wide. The highway will replace Adams Boulevard which in recent years has often been congested.

1. What will be built?
   (A) A new highway
   (B) An airport
   (C) A new boulevard

2. Where is the airport?
   (A) Downtown
   (B) In the suburbs
   (C) 6 miles away

3. How wide will the highway be?
   (A) 6 miles
   (B) 6 lanes
   (C) 10 miles

4. What has been the problem with Adams Boulevard?
   (A) It's often congested.
   (B) It's not long enough.
   (C) It's not busy enough.

3. Read the following paragraph and answer the questions.

> The Center for Urban Living opens today. The Center offers a unique combination of residential, recreational and professional spaces. It will contain apartments, city government offices, a theater, a concert hall, a grocery store, a stadium and a museum. The Center is located on major bus and subway lines. Parking is available in the Center's underground lots.

1. Where is the Center?
   (A) In an urban area
   (B) In the suburbs
   (C) In the country

2. Which is NOT found in the Center?
   (A) Apartments
   (B) A museum
   (C) A hospital

3. How can you reach the Center?
   (A) By subway
   (B) By plane
   (C) By boat

4. Where can you park at the Center?
   (A) Behind the stadium
   (B) In underground lots
   (C) On the roof

This view of a city is called its "skyline."

9 | BANKS

WORDS TO KNOW

ATM	checking account	interest	service charge
balance	currency	lend	teller
bank statement	debt	loan	teller window
borrow	deposit	percent	transaction
cash	deposit slip	receipt	withdrawal
checkbook	fee	savings account	withdrawal slip

WORD PRACTICE

1. Write the words under the appropriate category.

teller	checkbook	deposit slip
currency	service charge	customer
bank manager	cash	withdrawal slip
interest	bank slip	balance

PEOPLE

TELLER

MONEY

CURRENCY

FORM

CHECKBOOK

2. Use the words from the Words to Know section to complete the sentences.

1. People can write checks to pay for their purchases if there is money in their _C_ _H_ _E_ _C_ _K_ _I_ _N_ _G_ account.

2. One service of a bank is _L_ _E_ _ _ _ _ _ _ _ _G_ money.

3. Identification is required when _C_ _ _ _ _ _ _ _ _G_ a check.

4. _W_ _ _ _T_ _H_ _ _ _ _ _ _ _ _I_ _N_ _G_ money from your account will reduce your savings.

5. _B_ _ _ _ _ _ _ _ _E_ _D_ money must be repaid.

6. People often do their banking at an _ _ _T_ _ (automated teller machine).

40   Banks

3. Look at this bank statement and answer the questions.

1st Federal Bank	Statement	April, 1993
John Doe	CHECKING ACCOUNT	
	Balance Last Month	+ 642.00
4/09/91	Deposit	+ 106.00
4/09/91	Check #432	- 4.75
4/10/91	Check #433	- 13.00
4/20/91	Service Charge	- 40.00
4/21/91	Deposit	+ 208.00
4/22/91	Interest	+ 6.42
4/30/91	Balance	904.67

1. How many checks were written in April? _TWO_

2. What was last month's balance? _____

3. What is the balance for April? _____

4. How much interest was added to the account? _____

5. How much was the service charge? _____

4. Fill in the blanks.

To put money in the bank, fill out a _D E P O S I T_ slip.

To take money out of a bank, fill out a _W _ _ _ D _ _ _ _ L_ slip.

Take the slips to the _T _ _ L E R_ . The teller stands behind the

_T E _ _ _ _ '_ W _ _ D O _ . The teller will give you your

_B _ _ _ _ _ _ after your _T R A N S _ _ _ _ _ _ _ .

5. Look at this check and answer the questions.

```
                                                    546
1 ST FEDERAL BANK    Oct 5, 1994 _____

Pay to the Order of  District Loan Co. _____  [ $55.00 ]
Sum  Fifty-five and• • • • • •  00/100 dollars

Memo: Car Loan Payment _____    J Doe _____
```

1. Who wrote the check? _J. DOE_

2. To whom was the check written? _____

3. When was the check written? _____

4. How much was the check for? _____

5. What is the check for? _____

6. What is the check number? _____

6. Draw a line between opposites.

cash —————————————— customer
teller ——————————————check
deposit   service charge
interest   borrow
lend   withdrawal

7. Write the *-ing* form of the following verbs.

1. cash   _CASHING_

2. lend   _____

3. withdraw   _____

4. check   _____

5. bank   _____

6. borrow   _____

READING PRACTICE

1. Which underlined word is incorrect?

GRAMMAR TO KNOW:	
conditional sentences	gerunds
prepositions	infinitives

1. If you would like <u>to</u> make <u>a</u> deposit, you must <u>filled</u> out a bank slip.
   　　　　　　　A　　　　　B　　　　　　　　　ⓒ

2. There <u>is</u> a small service charge <u>for</u> <u>cashed</u> a check.
   　　　A　　　　　　　　　　　　　B　　C

3. Would you like <u>making</u> a withdrawal <u>from</u> <u>your</u> savings account?
   　　　　　　　　A　　　　　　　　　　B　　C

4. There <u>is</u> a high rate <u>in</u> interest <u>on</u> this loan.
   　　　A　　　　　　　B　　　　　C

5. If you <u>are</u> in debt, this bank will <u>lent</u> you money <u>at</u> a rate of eight percent.
   　　　　　A　　　　　　　　　　　　B　　　　　　　C

6. Your balance <u>will</u> be <u>displayed</u> <u>at</u> your deposit receipt.
   　　　　　　　A　　　　B　　　C

7. The teller <u>said</u> I should <u>contact</u> the branch manager <u>inquire</u> about loans.
   　　　　　　A　　　　　　　B　　　　　　　　　　　　C

8. There <u>is</u> a penalty <u>to</u> early withdrawal <u>from</u> this account.
   　　　A　　　　　　B　　　　　　　　　　C

9. Joan wanted <u>balanced</u> her checkbook but <u>realized</u> that she had <u>lost</u> a
   　　　　　　　　A　　　　　　　　　　　　B　　　　　　　　　C
   check.

2. Read the following conversation and answer the questions.

Customer:	I need a loan. I want to buy a house.
Bank officer:	Do you have any debts?
Customer:	I have a $3,000 car loan and a $10,000 school loan.
Bank officer:	How much do you want to borrow?
Customer:	Can you lend me $100,000?

1. What does the customer want?
   (A) A withdrawal slip
   (B) A savings account
   (C) A loan

2. Why does the customer need money?
   (A) She wants to buy a house.
   (B) She needs a new car.
   (C) She wants to go to school.

3. How many loans does the customer have?
   (A) 1
   (B) 2
   (C) 3

4. How much does she want to borrow?
   (A) $3,000
   (B) $10,000
   (C) $100,000

3. Read the following paragraph and answer the questions.

> A checking account is convenient. You can easily pay your bills with checks. Your paycheck can be deposited directly into your checking account. But many people prefer to keep their money in a savings account because a savings account earns interest. This interest can be between 5% to 8% or more. A checking account usually does not offer interest.

1. What is good about a checking account?
   (A) It is profitable.
   (B) It is convenient.
   (C) It is free.

2. Why do some people prefer savings accounts?
   (A) They have little money.
   (B) They hate checks.
   (C) They like to receive interest.

3. What can be deposited into a checking account?
   (A) A bill
   (B) A paycheck
   (C) A service charge

4. How high can interest be?
   (A) Only 8%
   (B) Less than 8%
   (C) More than 8%

FORMS OF MONEY

Credit Card

Bills

Coins

10 RESTAURANTS

WORDS TO KNOW

ashtray	cup	menu	smoking section
bar	dessert	napkin	snack
bartender	diner	order	soft drink
bill	dinner	placemat	spoon
breakfast	fork	plate	supper
cafe	glass	reservation	tablecloth
captain	knife	saucer	tip
check	lunch	service	waiter
coffee	meal	silverware	waitress

WORD PRACTICE

1. Complete the following sentences.

1. It is good to eat <u>B R E A K F A S T</u> in the morning.

2. At busy restaurants a <u>R _ _ _ _ V _ _ _ _ _</u> is necessary.

3. A <u>B _ _ T _ _ _ _ _</u> serves drinks at the bar.

4. The <u>L _ _ _ _</u> hour falls between 11:30 and 1:00 p.m.

5. A 15% <u>S _ _ _ _ _ E</u> charge is added to the bill.

2. Write which meal or snack is usually eaten 1st, 2nd, 3rd, and 4th.

CHOICES: dinner, afternoon snack, breakfast, lunch

1st meal   <u>BREAKFAST</u>

2nd meal   _____

3rd meal   _____

4th meal   _____

3. Write the appropriate adjective.

CHOICES: dirty, slow, cold, high, smoky

1. This coffee is _____ _COLD_ _____.

2. This bill is too _____ .

3. The service is very _____ .

4. The spoon is _____ .

5. The smoking section is very _____ .

4. Complete the following items you put on a table.

1. _S A L T_ and _P E P P E R   S H A K E R S_

2. _N_ _ _ _ _ _

3. _G_ _ _ _ _S_

4. _S_ _ _ _ _ _

5. _P_ _ _ _ _E_

6. _F_ _ _ _

7. _K_ _N_ _ _ _

8. _P_ _L_ _ _ _ _ _M_ _ _

5. Write the correct word in the blank for each of the definitions below.

ashtray   soft drink   smoking section   tip
check   snack   waitress   silverware

1. A container for cigarette ashes   _ASHTRAY_ _____

2. A sweet carbonated drink _____

3. A woman who serves food _____

4. An area for people who smoke _____

5. Food eaten between meals _____

6. A bill for restaurant meals _____

7. Extra money for the waiter or waitress _____

8. Knives, forks, spoons, etc. _____

6. Circle the correct adverb of frequency.

1. A waiter ((always) / never) takes an order.

2. Restaurants (never / always) have tables.

3. A reservation is (always / sometimes) necessary for dinner.

4. Customers should (sometimes / never) leave without tipping.

5. Napkins are (sometimes / always) made of paper.

READING PRACTICE

1. Which underlined word is incorrect? Circle the letter.

GRAMMAR TO KNOW:	
conjunctions	modal auxiliaries
pronouns	subject-verb agreement

1. I will like to order a cup of coffee with my breakfast, please.
   (A)   B   C

2. Bill looked at the menu a long time while then ordered only coffee.
          A   B   C

3. Puts your cigarette out, please. This is not the smoking section.
   A   B   C

4. The waitress, hoping her would get a big tip, put the check on the table.
                 A   B   C

5. This restaurant is busy and would only seat parties with a reservation.
                     A   B   C

6. Let's has a late-night snack at the diner.
   A   B   C

7. Waiter, there is a spot on my spoon, but this tablecloth is filthy!
                  A   B   C

8. He should always use a small fork when eating your salad.
   A   B   C

9. The bartender enjoys talking to people who are on your lunch break.
                 A   B   C

10. This restaurant are famous for its selection of rich desserts.
                     A   B   C

2. Read the following conversation and answer the questions.

Waiter:	I hope you have enjoyed your meal.
Customer:	It was very good.
Waiter:	Would you like to see the dessert menu?
Customer:	No, thank you. But I would like a cup of coffee.
Waiter:	Fine. Anything else?
Customer:	No... could you bring my check with the coffee?
Waiter:	Certainly.

1. The customer has just finished his
   (A) coffee
   (B) dessert
   (C) meal

2. What does the waiter offer the customer?
   (A) A cup of coffee
   (B) The dessert menu
   (C) His check

3. When does the customer want his check?
   (A) After his coffee
   (B) Before his coffee
   (C) With his coffee

4. After the customer finishes his coffee, he will
   (A) pay the check
   (B) order a meal
   (C) have dessert

3. Read the following and answer the questions.

When diners in a restaurant finish their meal, they pay their check, leave a tip, and go. The waiter quickly prepares the table for other customers. He first takes away the dirty dishes and napkins. He then changes the tablecloth. He cleans out the ashtray and places it in the center of the table with the salt and pepper. Finally, he places clean plates, glasses, and silverware on the table.

1. How does the waiter work?
   (A) Slowly
   (B) Quickly
   (C) Carelessly

2. Why does he remove the dishes?
   (A) They are ready.
   (B) They are dirty.
   (C) They are new.

3. What does the waiter change?
   (A) The ashtray
   (B) The chairs
   (C) The tablecloth

4. Where does the waiter put the clean ashtray?
   (A) On another table
   (B) Next to the salt and pepper
   (C) On top of the napkin

11 ENTERTAINMENT

WORDS TO KNOW

actor/actress	classical	music	program
aisle	comedian	musical	rock
attend	comedy	musician	row
audience	conductor	opera	seat
balcony	concert	orchestra	singer
box	director	performer	stage
cast	drama	play	star
chorus	film	playhouse	symphony
circus	intermission	popcorn	theater
cinema	movie	popular	ticket

WORD PRACTICE

1. Write the noun for the person which matches the verb.

VERB   NOUN

1. conduct   _CONDUCTOR_

2. direct   _____

3. act   _____ or _____

4. perform   _____

5. sing   _____

2. Cross out the word in each of the following groups that does NOT belong.

1. music: opera   symphony   ~~seat~~
2. theater: play   television   movie
3. cast: actor   laughter   actress
4. seat: balcony   music   row
5. perform: sit   act   sing

3. Circle the words below for types of entertainment. (7 words)

(concert)	ticket	seat	movie
box	opera	musical	row
symphony	play	intermission	comedy

4. Fill in the blanks.

Music

There are many kinds of musical entertainment. One kind is
_C_ _L_ _A_ _S_ _S_ _I_ _C_ _A_ _L_ ; two examples of this kind of music are the
_S_ _ _ _ _ _ _ _Y_ and the _O_ _ _ _ _A_ . Another kind of
musical entertainment is the _M_ _ _ _ _ _ _L_ play, which is more
popular than opera. Most popular of all is _R_ _ _ _K_.

5. Draw a line between words that are the same or similar in meaning.

1. opera   concert
2. film   conductor
3. symphony   play
4. drama   actress
5. director   musical
6. star   movie

6. Write the word under the appropriate category.

	PERSON	ACTION	LOCATION
actor	ACTOR		
attend		ATTEND	
audience			
balcony			BALCONY
box			
cast			
chorus			
cinema			
conduct			
direct			
musician			
perform			

7. Complete the following questions.

CHOICES: playhouse, cast, row, chorus

1. What is an _I N T E R M I S S I O N_?
   A break between acts in a play

2. What is a _____ ?
   The entire company of performers in a performance

3. What is a _____ ?
   A group of singers and dancers who do not have major parts

4. What is a _____ ?
   A section of seats running between aisles

5. What is a _____ ?
   A small theatre

READING PRACTICE

1. Which underlined word is incorrect? Circle the letter.

> **GRAMMAR TO KNOW:**
> conjunctions   gerunds
> infinitives   prepositions

1. We <u>were</u> lucky to <u>getting</u> box seats <u>for</u> Friday's concert.
       A   Ⓑ   C

2. Would you like to go <u>see</u> a movie at the cinema <u>nor</u> a play <u>at</u> the theater?
                      A   B   C

3. Scott <u>listens</u> to rock music, <u>but</u> his parents enjoy <u>to listen</u> to classical
         A   B   C

   music.

4. <u>My</u> favorite actress <u>is</u> <u>at</u> the chorus in this old movie.
     A   B C

5. The star <u>to perform</u> currently in this opera <u>is</u> <u>a</u> former dramatic actor.
           A   B C

6. <u>The</u> conductor <u>in</u> the city's symphony orchestra is well-<u>known</u>.
    A   B   C

7. Some musicians <u>perform</u> <u>pleasing</u> themselves <u>rather than</u> to please
              A   B   C

   their audience.

8. Most people <u>buy</u> popcorn <u>eating</u> during the intermission <u>of</u> the film.
          A   B   C

9. If you'd like <u>using</u> my tickets <u>for</u> the musical comedy, you <u>may</u>.
            A   B   C

10. We <u>have</u> fourth-row tickets <u>of</u> <u>the</u> circus tonight.
      A   B C

MUSICAL EXPRESSIONS

<u>Positive Expressions</u>
She sings like a bird.
She has a song in her heart.
She has a golden throat.

<u>Negative Expressions</u>
She has a voice like a bull frog.
She can't carry a tune.
She couldn't carry a tune in a bucket.
She's tone deaf.
Her voice would shatter glass.

2. Read the following paragraph and answer the questions.

> Many people enjoy seeing movies in a theater. They pay for their tickets at the box office. Then they might buy some popcorn to eat during the movie. Before the movie begins, there are often advertisements for coming attractions.

1. Where do many people like to see movies?
   (A) At home
   (B) In a theater
   (C) On TV

2. Where do people get tickets for a movie?
   (A) At the box office
   (B) At their seats
   (C) From their friends

3. People at a movie sometimes eat
   (A) hot dogs
   (B) corn on the cob
   (C) popcorn

4. What are coming attractions?
   (A) Movies to be seen soon
   (B) Unwanted guests
   (C) Magnets

3. Read the following conversation and answer the questions.

> John: Let's see a Broadway play while we're visiting New York next month.
> Mary: Theater tickets are too expensive.
> John: We can get cheap seats—in the balcony, for instance.
> Mary: Okay, but we'd better buy our tickets soon. Broadway shows are often sold out weeks in advance.

1. When are they visiting New York?
   (A) Next week
   (B) Next month
   (C) Next year

2. What does John want to do in New York?
   (A) Go to a theater
   (B) See the Statue of Liberty
   (C) Attend a baseball game

3. Where are the cheap seats in a theater?
   (A) On Broadway
   (B) In the balcony
   (C) In the orchestra

4. Mary says that tickets for Broadway shows are often
   (A) easy to get
   (B) cheap
   (C) sold out

12 POST OFFICE

WORDS TO KNOW

address	letter	postal clerk	sort
air	mailbox	postal code	special delivery
counter	mail carrier	postcard	stamp
deliver	overnight mail	postmark	surface
envelope	package	post office box	weigh
first class	parcel post	return address	window
label	postage	seal	zip code

WORD PRACTICE

1. Complete these sentences.

1. The mail is delivered by the _P O S T_ _O F F I C E_.

2. This _L_ _ _ _ _ _R_ weighs 2 ounces.

3. A postcard needs a 25-cent _S_ _T_ _ _ _.

4. The postal _C_ _ _ _ _K_ stands behind a _C_ _ _ _ _T_ _E R_ in the post office.

5. The _P_ _ _ _ _M_ _ _ _ on this letter was July 15.

6. Send this package by _P_ _ _R_ _ _ _ post.

7. P.O.B. stands for post _O_ _ _ _ _ _ _ _B_ _ _.

8. In the United States, a postal code is called a _Z_ _ _ _ _C_ _ _ _ _.

9. The mailing _L_ _ _ _ _ tells the post office where to deliver the package.

10. A _F_ _ _ _ _ _ _C_ _L_ _ _ _ _ stamp costs more than a fourth class one.

2. Write six words or phrases that have '*post*' as part of the word or phrase.

1. _POSTAGE_   4. _____

2. _____   5. _____

3. _____   6. _____

3. Write these sentences in the correct order. What happens first?

I read the letter.   I write a reply.
I seal and stamp my letter.   I see my mail.
I open the envelope.   I put my reply into an envelope.
I look in my mail box.   I take it to the post office.

1. *I LOOK IN MY MAILBOX* _____

2. _____

3. _____

4. _____

5. _____

6. _____

7. _____

8. _____

4. Complete the sentences.

1. PROBLEM: The package must arrive tomorrow.

   SOLUTION: Send it _O_ _V_ _E_ _R_ _N_ _I_ _G_ _H_ _T_ mail.

2. PROBLEM: I don't know how much postage is required.

   SOLUTION: The postal clerk will _W_ _ _ _ _ the letter.

3. PROBLEM: My mail doesn't arrive at my home.

   SOLUTION: Use a _P_ _ _ _ _O_ _F_ _ _ _ _ box.

4. PROBLEM: This package is too heavy to send by air.

   SOLUTION: Send it _S_ _ _ _ _ _ _E_ mail.

5. PROBLEM: I don't know when this letter was sent.

   SOLUTION: Look at the _P_ _ _ _ _M_ _ _ _K_ on the

   envelope.

5. Label the parts of the envelope.

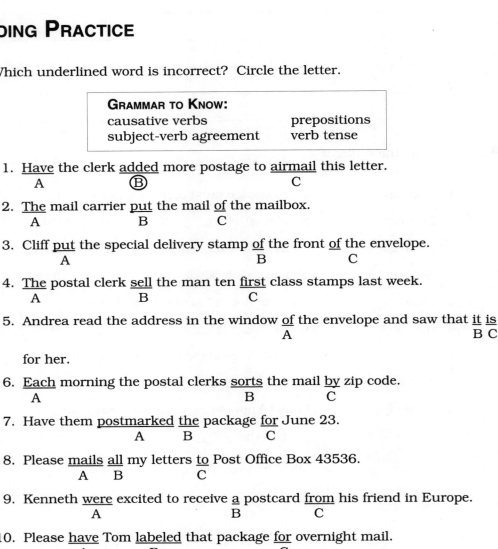

1. _RETURN ADDRESS_

2. _____

3. _____

4. _____

ACE COMPANY
500 Elm Ave.
Indianapolis, IN 50312

Mr. John A. Smith
500 12th Street
New York, NY 10012

READING PRACTICE

1. Which underlined word is incorrect? Circle the letter.

> **GRAMMAR TO KNOW:**
> causative verbs   prepositions
> subject-verb agreement   verb tense

1. <u>Have</u> the clerk <u>added</u> more postage to <u>airmail</u> this letter.
    A   Ⓑ   C

2. <u>The</u> mail carrier <u>put</u> the mail <u>of</u> the mailbox.
   A   B   C

3. Cliff <u>put</u> the special delivery stamp <u>of</u> the front <u>of</u> the envelope.
     A   B   C

4. <u>The</u> postal clerk <u>sell</u> the man ten <u>first</u> class stamps last week.
   A   B   C

5. Andrea read the address in the window <u>of</u> the envelope and saw that <u>it</u> <u>is</u>
                                A   B C

for her.

6. <u>Each</u> morning the postal clerks <u>sorts</u> the mail <u>by</u> zip code.
   A   B   C

7. Have them <u>postmarked</u> <u>the</u> package <u>for</u> June 23.
           A   B   C

8. Please <u>mails</u> <u>all</u> my letters <u>to</u> Post Office Box 43536.
      A   B   C

9. Kenneth <u>were</u> excited to receive <u>a</u> postcard <u>from</u> his friend in Europe.
      A   B   C

10. Please <u>have</u> Tom <u>labeled</u> that package <u>for</u> overnight mail.
     A   B   C

2. Read the following conversation and answer the questions.

Customer:	I'd like to mail this package to Hong Kong.
Postal Clerk:	How would you like to send it? By air or surface?
Customer:	By air. A boat would take too long.
Postal Clerk:	It's very heavy. Why don't you send it parcel post by air? It will take 2 weeks and be less expensive.
Customer:	No, I want to send it overnight. It must be there tomorrow.

1. What is the customer doing?
   (A) Mailing a letter
   (B) Taking a boat
   (C) Sending a package

2. What is wrong with surface mail?
   (A) It's too expensive.
   (B) It's too slow.
   (C) It's unreasonable.

3. What service does the clerk recommend?
   (A) Parcel post by air
   (B) Special delivery
   (C) First Class

4. When must the package arrive?
   (A) This afternoon
   (B) Tomorrow
   (C) After 2 weeks

3. Read the following announcement and answer the questions.

> ADVICE FROM YOUR POST OFFICE:
> When addressing an envelope, it is important to write clearly. Addresses are often read by machine and sorted by zip code. You must have the correct postage and your return address on every envelope.

1. When is it important to write clearly?
   (A) When writing your mother
   (B) When taking a test
   (C) When addressing an envelope

2. How are envelopes sorted?
   (A) By zip code
   (B) By return address
   (C) By date

3. How much postage is required?
   (A) None if mailed early
   (B) Double the required amount
   (C) The correct amount

4. What is required on every envelope?
   (A) Insufficient postage
   (B) A return address
   (C) Today's postmark

13 THE GAS STATION

WORDS TO KNOW

air	fill (it) up	gas tank	repair
air pump	fix	grease	spare tire
car	flat tire	hood	tire
change the oil	gas	jack	trunk
check the oil	gas pump	mechanic	wheel
engine	gas station	oil change	windshield

WORD PRACTICE

1. Complete the sentences.

1. The _E_ _N_ _G_ _I_ _N_ _E_ is located under the _H_ _ _ _D_ .

2. Make sure the _T_ _ _ _ _S_ have enough _A_ _ _ .

3. The _W_ _ _ _ _S_ _ _ _ _ _D_ should be kept clean.

4. If the _G_ _ _ _T_ _ _ _K_ is empty, _F_ _ _ _L_ it _ _ .

5. The spare tire is in the _T_ _ _ _ _ _ .

2. Cross out the word that does NOT belong.

1. gas   oil   ~~coins~~

2. hood   paper   windshield

3. wheel   tire   rain

4. fill it up   take a break   check the oil

5. jack   oil   flat tire

3. Draw a line between a word and its definition.

NOUN	DEFINITION
windshield	gas station
service station	front window of a car
gas	fix a problem
repair	car repairman
mechanic	fuel

4. What can a driver get for his car at a gas station? Circle the 4 words.

ink   (gas)   cream   vinegar

oil   bread   grease   air

5. Write the simple form of the verb.

1. filling up   _FILL UP_____ the tank.

2. changing   _____ the oil.

3. checking   _____ the tires.

4. pumping   _____ the gas.

5. repairing   _____ the engine.

6. Circle the correct verb form.

1. I (filling the car up / (fill the car up)) with gas when the gas tank is empty.

2. The service station attendant is (changing / change) the oil now.

3. You should (check / checking) the air pressure of your tires.

4. A service station attendant (pumps / pumping) gas for a living.

5. The mechanic is (repair / repairing) the engine today.

7. Complete the sentences.

CHOICES: change, tire, oil, trunk, hood

1. I have a flat tire.

   I need to change the _____*TIRE*_____ .

2. The oil is low. It's down a quart.

   I need to add some _____ .

3. The oil is dirty. I haven't changed it for 15,000 miles.

   I need to _____ the oil.

4. The mechanic wants to check the oil.

   He must check under the _____ .

5. I have a flat tire.

   The spare one is in the _____ .

8. Label the parts of the car.

CHOICES: hood, tire, trunk, windshield

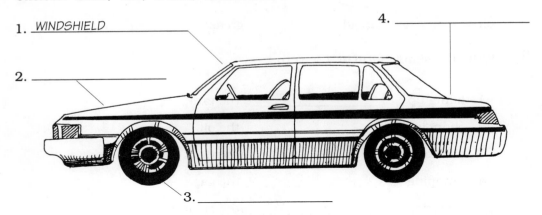

1. _WINDSHIELD_

2. _____

3. _____

4. _____

READING PRACTICE

1. Which underlined word is incorrect? Circle the letter.

> **GRAMMAR TO KNOW:**
> infinitives   adverbs of frequency
> modal auxiliaries   subject-verb agreement

1. To prevent <u>a</u> flat tire, you <u>do</u> put air in your tires <u>regularly</u>.
        A   Ⓑ   C

2. Lori took <u>the</u> car <u>to</u> the gas station <u>filling</u> it up.
          A   B   C

3. Steven <u>used</u> the jack to raise the tire <u>off</u> the ground <u>changing</u> it.
          A   B   C

4. Marilyn <u>once a week</u> checks <u>the</u> oil in <u>her</u> car.
            A   B   C

5. The mechanic <u>walk</u> up to <u>the</u> gas pump to <u>help</u> the customer.
           A   B   C

6. If <u>your</u> car needed repair, you <u>will</u> have asked a mechanic <u>for</u> help.
  A   B   C

7. Bill opened <u>the</u> hood of the car <u>seeing</u> what was wrong <u>with</u> the engine.·
            A   B   C

8. There <u>are</u> a spare tire <u>in</u> the trunk <u>of</u> my car.
      A   B   C

9. There <u>are</u> grease <u>on</u> the engine <u>of</u> my car.
      A   B   C

10. The tires <u>of</u> my old car <u>once a year</u> need <u>to be</u> replaced.
     A   B   C

2. Read the following paragraph and answer the questions.

> Many service station customers today pump their own gas. This is a recent change. A few years ago, a service station attendant would put gas in your car, check the oil, and clean your windshield. Now, if you pump your own gas, you save money. If a service station attendant pumps your gas or checks your oil, it costs you more money.

1. Many customers at gas stations today
   (A) pump their own gas
   (B) use less gas
   (C) have small cars

2. What does the station attendant do to your oil?
   (A) Checks it
   (B) Cooks with it
   (C) Pumps it

3. Why do customers pump their own gas?
   (A) To learn how
   (B) To save money
   (C) To choose the right gas

4. When did customers start pumping their own gas?
   (A) Only recently
   (B) In the summer
   (C) During vacation

3. Read the following conversation and answer the questions.

> Station Attendant: Your car needed oil. We put in a quart of oil.
> Customer: Is that the only problem? I was afraid it was something more serious.
> Station Attendant: Everything seems OK. Make sure that the oil doesn't get too low.
> Customer: OK. How much do I owe you?
> Station Attendant: $12.50 plus $1.42 tax. That's $13.92 total.

1. What was the problem with the car?
   (A) It was old.
   (B) It needed oil.
   (C) It was out of gas.

2. What will the customer do next?
   (A) Repair the car
   (B) Add oil
   (C) Pay the bill

3. How much oil did the attendant put in the car?
   (A) A gallon
   (B) A quart
   (C) An ounce

4. How much was the tax?
   (A) $12.50
   (B) $13.92
   (C) $1.42

Unit Activities

Start Talking

1. **A Tour Guide (Class or Partners)**

   A friend is coming to visit you. Name all the "tourist" things to do or see where you live now (or in your hometown).

2. **City Planners (Class)**

   With your class, draw a plan for a new city. Name the streets, avenues, roads, highways, etc. Are there parks, rivers, harbors, etc.? Label the important
   buildings (schools, post offices, police and fire stations) and places (parking garages, stores and gas stations.)

3. **Weekend Errands (Partners)**

   Name three things you have to do on Saturday. Exchange your list with your partner. Add three more things.

   Look at the city map you drew with your class. Tell your partner where to go.

Errand	Plan
Laundry	Go to dry cleaners on _____ (street).
Buy clothes	Go to the department store.
Mail books home	Go to the Post Office.

Put It in Writing

1. Write a description of the city where you live. Write about the good things and write about the bad things.

   Give your description to your classmate. Your classmate adds two words to your description. Hint: The words can be added at the beginning, middle, or end of a sentence.

   Give this description to another classmate. Add two sentences to the new description. Hint: The sentences can be added at the beginning, middle, or end of the description.

   Return the description to the original writer. Rewrite your own description.

ACT IT OUT 1

Functions
Giving directions
Asking for directions
Associating places with purposes
Sequencing events

Characters
Stranger 1
Stranger 2
Citizen 1
Citizen 2
Citizen 3

Setting:
Two people in a car stop a stranger on the street and ask for directions. Two passers-by stop to offer advice.

Stranger 1:	Excuse me.
Citizen 1:	Yes. Can I help you?
Stranger 1:	Yes, please. We're lost.
Citizen 1:	Where do you want to go?
Stranger 1:	I want to get something to eat.
Stranger 2:	And I want to buy stamps.
Stranger 1:	And I need to get gas.
Stranger 2:	But first I want to change money.
Citizen 1:	Hmmmmmm.
Citizen 2:	What's the problem?
Citizen 1:	She wants to go to the gas station.
	Then he wants to go to the bank.
	Then she wants to go to the post office.

	And then they both want to go to a restaurant.
Citizen 2:	Hmmmmmm.
Citizen 3:	What's going on?
Citizen 2:	First, she wants to go to a restaurant.
	Then, he wants to go to the bank.
	Then they both want to go to the post office.
	And then she wants to go to the gas station.
Stranger 1:	No, first I want to get gas.
	Then, I want to go to a restaurant.
Stranger 2:	And I want to change money first. Then I want to buy stamps.
Citizen 3:	That's easy.
	First, go straight on Maple Street. The gas station is 4 blocks away — on the corner of First and Maple.
	Then turn right on First Street and go 2 blocks. Park your car in the lot on the corner of Third and Elm.
	Then walk across the street to the bank.
	The post office is next to the bank on the right side.
	And the restaurant is around the corner on Elm Street.
Strangers:	Thank you very much.
Citizens:	Have a nice day.

ACT IT OUT 2

Do the skit again with new purposes. Use the City Plan your class drew in **Start Talking** to give directions.

Warm Up

Need	Action	Location
I want _____.	I want to go to _____	The _____ is _____.
gas	gas station	
food	grocery store	
stamps	post office	
a book	library	
...	...	

Words Used by Real People

Hmmmmmm
Hmmmmm is a sound that means you are thinking. *Hmmmmm*

Hmmmmm is a sound that means you are interested. *Hmmmmm*

ON THE ROAD

How many words from this unit can you identify. Write the words on the lines. Draw lines from the picture to the words.

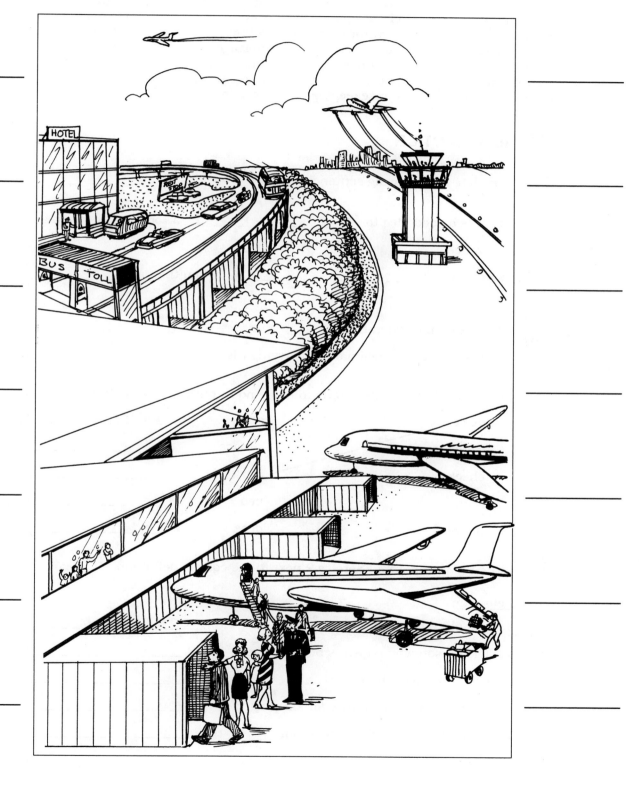

14 | HOTEL SERVICE

WORDS TO KNOW

bellman	elevator	key	reservation
check in	elevator operator	lobby	reserve
check out	floor	luggage	room
desk clerk	front desk	maid	room service
doorman	guest	make up	suite
double bed	housekeeping	register	towel

WORD PRACTICE

1. Complete the following sentences.

1. It is a good idea to _R E S E R V E_ a room in a hotel in advance.

2. Guests _R_ _ _ _ _ _ _ _R_ when they _C_ _ _ _ _ _L_ _ .

3. Guests pay when they _C_ _ _ _ _ _ _ _ _ .

4. Guests tip the bellman for carrying the _L U_ _ _ _ _ _ .

2. Draw a line between the words to make noun phrases. Write the noun phrase.

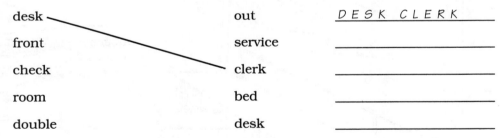

desk	out	_D E S K C L E R K_
front	service	_____
check	clerk	_____
room	bed	_____
double	desk	_____

3. Write the words from Exercise 2 next to the correct definition.

definition	word
1. The place to register at a hotel	_F R O N T D E S K_
2. The person who registers hotel guests	_____
3. Pay and leave a hotel	_____
4. A large piece of furniture for sleeping	_____
5. Food delivered to the hotel room	_____

4. Circle the correct word.

1. Guests meet their friends in the hotel (*desk* / (*lobby*)).
2. The (*key* / *bellman*) carries the bags.
3. The (*doorman* / *maid*) signals for a taxi.
4. The (*maid* / *clerk*) cleans the hotel rooms.
5. Large hotels usually have several (*luggage* / *elevators*).
6. I sat in the (*lobby* / *elevator*) and waited for my friend.
7. The bellman expected a larger (*floor* / *tip*).
8. Call (*room service* / *housekeeping*) to order breakfast.

5. Fill in the blanks.

At the Hotel

Last weekend I went to New York City. I had already made my

R E S E R V A T I O N S at the Nikko Hotel. When I

arrived, I C _ _ C _ _ _ _ I _ with the C _ _ _ _ standing at

the F _ _ _ _ D _ _ K . She R _ G _ _ _ _ _ _ E D me

and gave me a K _ _ . Then the B _ _ _ M _ _ carried my

L _ _ _ _ G _ upstairs to my S _ _ _ _ .

6. Write the word under the appropriate category.

	person	action	location
ballroom			B A L L R O O M
check out		C H E C K O U T	
clerk	C L E R K		
doorman			
elevator operator			
floor			
front desk			
guest			
lobby			
maid			
register			
reserve			
room			
suite			

7. What is the correct order for these actions? Number them from 1 to 8.

1. _____ The doorman opened the door for me.

2. _____ I registered at the front desk.

3. _1_ I arrived at the hotel.

4. _____ The bellman took me to the elevator.

5. _____ The elevator operator asked for my floor.

6. _____ I returned to the lobby.

7. _____ I tried the door to my suite.

8. _____ The key would not open the door.

READING PRACTICE

1. Which underlined word is incorrect? Circle the letter.

GRAMMAR TO KNOW:	
conditional sentences	conjunctions
modal auxiliaries	prepositions

1. The bellman should <u>carry</u> your luggage <u>to</u> your room if he is <u>ask</u>.
                       A   B   Ⓒ

2. Your reservation will be <u>cancelled</u> if you <u>didn't</u> check <u>in</u> before 6 p.m.
                              A   B   C

3. Hello, I <u>will</u> like to reserve a suite <u>with</u> a double bed <u>and</u> a view.
     A   B   C

4. Please <u>call</u> the front desk if you <u>needed</u> a key <u>for</u> your guests.
       A   B   C

5. Mrs. Connors <u>also</u> Mr. Shaw met <u>in</u> the lobby to <u>discuss</u> business.
             A   B   C

6. Please <u>wait</u> in the lobby <u>but</u> the doorman <u>calls</u> you a taxicab.
        A   B   C

7. The housekeeping staff <u>does</u> their work <u>of</u> the afternoons <u>while</u> everyone
                       A   B   C
is out.

8. This hotel <u>is</u> known <u>for</u> its beautiful lobby <u>also</u> large rooms.
         A   B   C

9. The maid <u>waited</u> until the guest left <u>but</u> <u>entered</u> the room.
       A   B   C

10. If you <u>see</u> a desk clerk, <u>asked</u> him if the hotel <u>requires</u> reservations.
       A   B   C

2. Read the following conversation and answer the questions.

Maid:	Good morning. I'm from Housekeeping. May I clean the room?
Guest:	Please come in. I'm checking out now.
Maid:	In that case, I'll just leave these towels. I'll come back later and prepare the room for the next guest.
Guest:	I'll be gone in 10 minutes.

1. What time of day is it?
   (A) Morning
   (B) Afternoon
   (C) Evening

2. Why is the maid there?
   (A) To turn down the bed
   (B) To deliver breakfast
   (C) To clean the room

3. What did the maid leave?
   (A) Keys
   (B) Towels
   (C) Luggage

4. When will the guest leave?
   (A) Tomorrow morning
   (B) Later in the evening
   (C) In 10 minutes

3. Read the following paragraph and answer the questions.

> When a taxi arrives at a hotel, a doorman opens the door for the passengers. He gets their luggage and takes them through the lobby to the front desk. The bellman waits by the front desk. He shows the guests their rooms and carries their luggage.

1. Who opens the taxi door?
   (A) The driver
   (B) The passengers
   (C) The doorman

2. The doorman escorts the guests through
   (A) the dining room
   (B) the lobby
   (C) the elevator

3. Where does the bellman wait?
   (A) By the front desk
   (B) By the front door
   (C) Near the elevator

4. Who shows the guests their rooms?
   (A) The doorman
   (B) The bellman
   (C) The elevator operator

15 PLANES

WORDS TO KNOW

airport	direct	nonsmoking	round trip
air traffic control	economy class	section	runway
arrival	flight	on time	smoking
board	flight attendant	one way	steward
coach	first class	overhead bin	stewardess
control tower	gate	passenger	take off
co-pilot	hand luggage	passport	tail
customs	jet	pilot	taxi
departure	land	plane	ticket agent
deplane	layover	reservation clerk	wing

WORD PRACTICE

1. Word Family: Write the noun form of the verb.

   VERB   NOUN

   1. fly   The _____FLIGHT_____ to Paris leaves at noon.

   2. depart   Our _____ has been delayed an hour.

   3. board   There were 68 passengers on _____ .

   4. arrive   The _____ of Flight 56 is delayed.

   5. reserve We made a _____ in first class.

   6. smoke   This is the _____ section.

   7. drive   The bus _____ helped load the luggage.

2. Draw a line between words that are opposites.

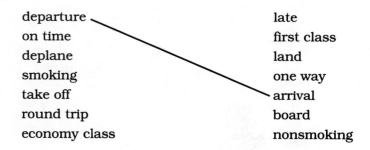

departure   late
on time   first class
deplane   land
smoking   one way
take off   arrival
round trip   board
economy class   nonsmoking

3. Complete the sentences.

1. Before boarding a plane, we line up at the _G_ _A_ _T_ _E_ .

2. For international travel, a _P_ _ _ _ _ _ _P_ _ _ _ _T_ is necessary.

3. Hand luggage is stowed in the _O_ _V_ _ _ _ _ _H_ _ _ _ _D_ bins.

4. A plane takes off on a _R_ _ _ _ _A_ _ .

5. International travelers must pass through _C_ _ _ _ _T_ _ _ _ _S_ .

4. Cross out the word that does NOT belong.

1. taxi	~~smoking~~	plane	bus
2. passenger	pilot	lawyer	flight attendant
3. tail	wing	engine	station
4. passport	dining car	customs	luggage
5. station	airport	bus stop	coins
6. luggage	late	early	on time

5. Write the word under the appropriate category.

	PERSON	PLACE
airport		_AIRPORT_
coach		
control tower		
co-pilot	_CO-PILOT_	
economy class		
flight attendant		
gate		
overhead bin		
passenger		
pilot		
plane		
runway		
ticket agent		
reservation clerk		

6. Write the job title next to the job description.

JOB TITLE   JOB DESCRIPTION

1. _TICKET AGENT_   A person who sells tickets

2. _____   A person who sits in the air traffic

                                             control and helps a plane land

3. _____   A person who makes travel

                                             reservations

4. _____   A person who flies a plane

5. _____   A person who helps passengers

                                             during a flight

READING PRACTICE

1. Which underlined word is incorrect? Circle the letter.

┌───┐
│ **GRAMMAR TO KNOW:**   │
│ infinitives   prepositions   │
│ subject-verb agreement   verb tense   │
└───┘

1. Pick up <u>your</u> luggage at baggage claim before you <u>went</u> <u>through</u> customs.
       A   Ⓑ   C

2. I <u>would</u> like <u>buying</u> a one-way first class ticket <u>to</u> Denver.
     A   B   C

3. The flight <u>to</u> Rome and Naples <u>are</u> <u>at</u> Gate 4 right now!
        A   B C

4. <u>Please</u> <u>stowing</u> your hand luggage <u>in</u> the overhead bin.
     A   B   C

5. You should <u>has</u> your passport ready <u>as</u> you <u>board</u> the plane.
           A   B   C

6. Jeff will <u>pick</u> you <u>up</u> <u>of</u> the airport.
        A   B C

7. The pilot will <u>informed</u> us <u>of</u> local weather as we <u>land</u>.
           A   B   C

8. If you wish <u>smoking</u>, please <u>sit</u> in <u>the</u> smoking section.
        A   B C

9. The flight attendant <u>told</u> us that <u>our</u> flight had been <u>cancel</u>.
          A   B   C

10. Please <u>tell</u> the ticket agent we <u>needs</u> two round trip tickets <u>to</u> Brussels.
        A   B   C

2. Read the following passage and answer the questions.

> After a plane lands, it taxis to the terminal. Passengers must stay in their seats with their seat belts fastened. They should keep their seat belts fastened until the plane has come to a stop at the terminal. The flight attendants will tell the passengers when it is safe to get up and remove their personal effects from the overhead bins. Passengers usually deplane from the forward exit.

1. What does a plane do after it lands?
   (A) Takes off
   (B) Taxis to the terminal
   (C) Changes direction

2. What must passengers do while a plane is taxiing?
   (A) Unfasten their seat belts
   (B) Remain in their seats
   (C) Remove their personal effects

3. What is stowed in the overhead bins?
   (A) Personal effects
   (B) Seat belts
   (C) Flight attendants

4. Where do passengers usually deplane?
   (A) The rear exit
   (B) Over the wing
   (C) The forward exit

3. Read the following conversation and answer the questions.

Flight Attendant:	You're in seat 3J, sir. In first class.
Passenger:	Is that seat in the smoking section?
Flight Attendant:	No, sir. This is a nonsmoking flight.
Passenger:	What time do we land in Tokyo?
Flight Attendant:	Flight time is approximately 14 hours. If we take off on time, we will land around 3:15 p.m.
Passenger:	Will my hand luggage fit in the overhead bin?
Flight Attendant:	If not, try under your seat.

1. Where is the passenger sitting?
   (A) In first class
   (B) In economy
   (C) In the smoking section

2. What are they travelling on?
   (A) A plane
   (B) A bus
   (C) A train

3. What is the passenger's destination?
   (A) Honolulu
   (B) Hong Kong
   (C) Tokyo

4. How long is the flight?
   (A) 3 hours
   (B) 14 hours
   (C) 15 hours

16 | TRAINS

WORDS TO KNOW

arrive	express	railroad	station
coach car	fare	reservation	ticket
conductor	local	reserve	timetable
depart	luggage	schedule	track
dining car	luggage rack	seat	trip
engineer	platform	snack bar	waiting room

WORD PRACTICE

1. Complete the questions.

1. Question: What is an _E N G I N E E R_?
   Answer: This person sits in the locomotive and drives the train.

2. Question: What is a _C _ _ _ _ _ _ _ R_?
   Answer: This person takes tickets on the train.

3. Question: What are _P _ _ _ _ _ _ _ R S_?
   Answer: These people ride the train.

4. Question: What is a _T _ _ _ _ _ _ _ _ __?
   Answer: This is a schedule of arrival and departure times.

5. Question: What is a _T _ _ _ K_?
   Answer: This is a metal rail that trains run on.

2. Fill in the blanks.

On the Train

You can _B O A R D_ a train after you buy a _T _ _ _ _ _ T_.

After the train leaves the station, a _C _ _ _ _ _ _ _ _ R_ will ask

you for your _T _ _ _ _ _ T_. On the train, you can usually get

something to eat at the _S _ _ _ _ B _ _ _ in the club car or in

the _D _ _ _ _ _ _ C _ _ .

3. Write the simple form of the following -ing forms.

1. departing _____DEPART_____
2. travelling _____
3. reserving _____
4. arriving _____
5. boarding _____

4. Write the word under the appropriate category.

	PERSON	ACTION	THING
arrive		*ARRIVE*	
board			
conductor	*CONDUCTOR*		
depart			
engineer			
reservation			*RESERVATION*
passenger			
ticket			
reserve			
timetable			

5. Complete the sentences.

1. I want to take the train to New York on Monday and return on Tuesday.

   I will buy a _R O U N D   T R I P_ ticket.

2. The local stops at every station. I want a faster train.

   I'll take the _E _ _ _ _ _ _ train.

3. You can sit anywhere in the coach car.

   The seats are not _R _ _ _ _ _ _ D_.

4. If you want a big dinner, you can eat in the dining car.

   If you are not very hungry, you can eat in the _S _ _ _ _

   _B _ _._

5. On the train you can put your luggage in the luggage rack.

   The _L _ _ _ _ _ _ _   R _ _ __ is usually over your

   _S _ _ _._

6. Write the word that matches the definition.

CHOICES: board, seat, schedule, passengers, gate, fare

1. train riders   _PASSENGERS_

2. price of a ride   _____

3. list of times   _____

4. get on the train   _____

5. entry to the platform   _____

6. place to sit   _____

7. Word Family. Write the appropriate form of the underlined word.

VERB	NOUN
arrive	arrival
depart	departure
reserve	reservation
board	boarding

1. The train <u>arrives </u>at 9:45.

   _____ARRIVAL_____ time is 9:45.

2. The train _____ at 10:00.

   <u>Departure </u> time is 10:00.

3. I <u>reserved</u> seats in the club car.

   I have a _____ in the club car.

4. We will _____ the train though Gate 6.

   <u>Boarding</u> is through Gate 6.

READING PRACTICE

1. Which underlined word is incorrect?

GRAMMAR TO KNOW:	
conjunctions	prepositions
subject-verb agreement	verb tense

1. When you <u>travel</u> by train, you <u>may</u> <u>ate</u> in the snack bar.
               A   B Ⓒ
2. What <u>are</u> the fare <u>for</u> a round trip ticket <u>to</u> New York?
          A   B   C
3. The local train <u>will</u> stop <u>at</u> every station, <u>still</u> the express will not.
                 A   B   C
4. <u>In</u> the coach car, you can <u>put</u> your luggage <u>of</u> the overhead luggage rack.
    A   B   C
5. Please <u>stays</u> <u>in</u> your seat so the conductor can <u>collect</u> your ticket.
         A B   C
6. We will <u>depart</u> Boston at 2:15 <u>or</u> arrive <u>in</u> New York at 4:20.
          A   B   C
7. <u>Looks</u> at the train timetable to <u>find out</u> what track your train will <u>be</u> on.
    A   B   C
8. The conductor will <u>tell</u> us when the train <u>is</u> about to <u>departing</u>.
               A   B   C
9. If the train does not <u>arrive</u> <u>on</u> schedule, you can wait <u>at</u> the waiting room.
               A B   C
10. If you <u>are</u> going <u>on</u> an overnight trip, you should always <u>calling</u> to reserve
         A   B   C
    your seat.

2. Read the following passage and answer the questions.

> Over a million people a day pass through Grand Central Station. The passengers can buy their tickets from the ticket agents, from a ticket machine, or from the conductor on the train.
>
> The passengers may wait in the waiting room for their trains. When the train is in the station, they pass through a gate to the train platform. They can board the train from the platform.
>
> On the train they can sit in the coach car (economy class) or club (first class). They can eat in the dining car or have a snack at the snack bar.

1. Where can passengers NOT buy their tickets?
    (A) From ticket agents
    (B) From the conductor
    (C) From soda machines

2. Where can passengers wait for a train?
    (A) In their hotel room
    (B) In a waiting room
    (C) In the coach car

3. Travellers in economy class will sit in
    (A) the club car
    (B) the coach car
    (C) the engine

4. Quick, short meals are available
    (A) at the snack bar
    (B) in the coach car
    (C) on the sidewalk

3. Read the following conversation and answer the questions.

> Passenger: Excuse me. Does this train stop at the Savoy station?
> Conductor: No, we go through that station. This is an express train. We don't stop there.
> Passenger: Oh, no! What should I do?
> Conductor: Get off at the next station which is Proctor City. You can get on the local train there.

1. Where does this conversation take place?
    (A) In a station
    (B) On a train
    (C) At a bus stop

2. Where does the passenger want to go?
    (A) To the end of the line
    (B) To Proctor City
    (C) To Savoy

3. Which train should the passenger have taken?
    (A) An express train
    (B) A local train
    (C) A night train

4. Where can the passenger catch the local?
    (A) Proctor City
    (B) In Savoy
    (C) Anywhere

17 CARS

WORDS TO KNOW

accelerator	engine	license plate	start
antenna	fill up	motor	station wagon
back up	fuel	passenger seat	steer
battery	gas	radiator	steering wheel
brake	gas tank	radio	taillight
brake light	glove compartment	rearview mirror	tire
bumper	headlight	reverse	trunk
convertible	hood	seat belt	turn signal
dashboard	hubcap	sedan	wheel
drive	ignition	spare tire	windshield
driver's seat	jack	speedometer	windshield wiper

WORD PRACTICE

1. Write the words that are found on the exterior of a car.

1. _H E A D L I G H T S_

2. _W _ _ D S _ _ _ _ D   W _ _ _ R S_

3. _T _ _ E S_

4. _W _ _ _ L S_

5. _B _ _ _ _ R S_

6. _T _ _ L L _ _ _ T S_

2. Draw a line between nouns that together make a new compound noun. Write the compound noun.

NOUN	+	NOUN	COMPOUND NOUN
tail		board	_TAILLIGHT_
dash		light	_____
wind		light	_____
head		shield	_____

3. There are more than one of these items on a car. Write the plural form.

SINGULAR		PLURAL	
1. bumper		two	_BUMPERS_
2. brake		four	
3. wheel		four	
4. seat belt		two or more	
5. seat		two or more	
6. headlight		two	
7. windshield wiper		two	
8. taillight		two	
9. tire		four	
10. turn signal		four	

4. Write the noun form for each of these verbs.

You will add either *-r*, *-er*, or *-or*.

VERB	NOUN	VERB	NOUN
1. drive	_D R I V E R_	4. accelerate	
2. bump		5. radiate	
3. wipe			

5. Draw a line between words that make a noun phrase. Write the noun phrase.

NOUN	+	NOUN	NOUN PHRASE
spare		mirror	_S P A R E T I R E_
steering		wheel	
windshield		seat	
passenger		wiper	
glove		signal	
turn		tire	
rearview		belt	
gas		plate	
license		compartment	
seat		tank	

6. Where would you most likely store these items? Write the words under the appropriate location.

	GLOVE COMPARTMENT	TRUNK
maps	*MAPS*	
luggage		*LUGGAGE*
spare tire		
extra change		
jack		
pencil		

READING PRACTICE

1. Which underlined word is incorrect? Circle the letter.

> **GRAMMAR TO KNOW:**
> causative verbs   modal auxiliaries
> prepositions   word families

1. Maria is always <u>carefully</u> not to <u>get</u> a flat tire <u>because</u> she has no spare.
   　　　　　　　　Ⓐ　　　　　　　B　　　　　　　　　C

2. <u>Because</u> <u>the</u> battery was dead, the engine <u>will</u> not start.
   　A　　　　B　　　　　　　　　　　　　　　　C

3. This new sedan <u>has</u> <u>a</u> large trunk and a <u>comfortably</u> driver's seat.
   　　　　　　　　A　B　　　　　　　　　　C

4. I will have Carrie <u>filling up</u> the gas tank <u>so</u> that you can <u>get</u> an early start.
   　　　　　　　　　A　　　　　　　　B　　　　　　C

5. <u>After</u> the accident, the car's rear bumper <u>and</u> taillights <u>will</u> not work.
   　A　　　　　　　　　　　　　　　　B　　　　　C

6. <u>I'll</u> have Steven <u>wore</u> his seat belt if he rides in the <u>passenger</u> seat.
   　A　　　　　　　B　　　　　　　　　　　　　C

7. If you keep an eye <u>in</u> your speedometer, you will <u>drive</u> at <u>the</u> proper speed.
   　　　　　　　　A　　　　　　　　　　　　B　　C

8. The speedometer <u>is</u> <u>convenient</u> located <u>on</u> the dashboard of the car.
   　　　　　　A　　B　　　　　　C

9. <u>Be</u> sure to have a mechanic <u>testing</u> the brakes, the engine <u>and</u> the steer-
   A　　　　　　　　　　　B　　　　　　　　　　　　　C
   ing before a long trip.

10. If you must drive <u>in</u> a rainy night, <u>check</u> the windshield wipers, the tires
   　　　　　　　　A　　　　　　　B
   <u>and</u> the brakes.
   　C

2. Read the following conversation and answer the questions.

Jane:	My car isn't old, but there's always something wrong with it.
Mel:	What now? Didn't you just have the brakes fixed?
Jane:	Yes. This time it seems to be the steering wheel. It's hard to turn.
Mel:	That could be dangerous. You'd better take it back to the mechanic.

1. The car is NOT
   (A) old
   (B) fast
   (C) small

2. What was recently repaired on the car?
   (A) The brakes
   (B) The hood
   (C) The wheels

3. What is hard to turn?
   (A) The rearview mirror
   (B) The steering wheel
   (C) The radio dial

4. Jane will probably
   (A) sell the car
   (B) not drive the car again
   (C) take the car to the mechanic

3. Read the following paragraph and answer the questions.

When you get ready to drive, there are several things to do before you start the car. Check the rearview mirror. Make sure you can see clearly out the back window. Put on your seat belt. Turn on the ignition; make sure that you have enough gas. Always accelerate slowly, and, most importantly, drive cautiously.

1. This passage gives advice on
   (A) starting to drive
   (B) parking a car
   (C) using a gas station

2. The purpose of the rearview mirror is to let you see
   (A) your face clearly
   (B) out the back window
   (C) straight ahead

3. Which of these in NOT mentioned in the passage?
   (A) Put on your seat belt.
   (B) Turn on the radio.
   (C) Accelerate slowly.

4. Which of the following is the MOST important?
   (A) Have a full tank of gas.
   (B) Keep your windows clean.
   (C) Drive cautiously.

18 ROADS

WORDS TO KNOW

beltway	honk	parkway	throughway
bridge	lane	pass	toll booth
bus	median	rest stop	trailer
circle	merge	route	truck
exit	motorbike	signal	turnpike
freeway	motorcycle	speed	van
highway	overpass	speed limit	yield

WORD PRACTICE

1. Write the appropriate words for different types of high-speed roads.

    1. A road that goes through a park land   _P_ _A_ _R_ _K_ _W_ _A_ _Y_

    2. A road without stop lights   _T_ _ _ _ _ _ _ _ _ _W_ _ _ _

    3. A road that goes around a city like a belt   _B_ _ _ _ _ _W_ _ _ _

    4. A road without intersections   _F_ _ _ _ _W_ _ _ _

    5. A general term for a high-speed road   _H_ _ _ _ _W_ _ _ _

2. Write the simple verb form of these *-ing* words.

    1. merging   _M E R G E_

    2. passing   _____

    3. driving   _____

    4. yielding   _____

    5. speeding   _____

    6. honking   _____

3. Fill in the blanks.

Passing on a Highway

You can go faster than the _S_ _P_ _E_ _E_ _D_ limit on a

_H_ _ _ _ _W_ _ _Y_ when you _P_ _ _ _S_ another car. Be sure to

leave lots of room and to use your turn _S_ _ _G_ _ _ _ _ .

4. Write the words under the appropriate category.

van	overpass	median
highway	truck	bus
trailer	motorcycle	yield
pass	honk	drive
merge	lane	rest stop

VEHICLE	ACTION	LOCATION
VAN	PASS	HIGHWAY
_____	_____	_____
_____	_____	_____
_____	_____	_____
_____	_____	_____

5. Fill in the blanks.

A Toll Road

Sometimes we must pay a _T_ _O_ _L_ _L_ to use some roads or bridges.

Some toll roads are called _T_ __ __ __ _P_ __ _K_ __ _S_ . We pay the

_T_ __ __ __ to people who sit in toll _B_ __ __ _T_ __ _S_ . Toll booths are

located at either the entrances to the turnpikes or the _E_ _X_ __ __ _S_

from the turnpikes.

6. What form of transportation do I need? Write the answer.

1. Forty people want a city tour.

   I need a _B_ _U_ _S_ .

2. I need to deliver a small package quickly during rush hour.

   I need a _M_ __ __ __ __ _B_ __ _K_ __ .

3. My family is taking a vacation in the mountains.

   I need a _T_ __ __ __ __ __ __ attached to my car.

4. I am moving my furniture to a new house.

   I need a _T_ __ __ __ __ .

5. I am taking my daughter's friends to the tennis match.

   I need a _V_ __ __ .

7. Draw a line between the nouns that make compound nouns. Write the compound noun next to it.

NOUN	+	NOUN	COMPOUND NOUN
1. belt		pass	_B E L T W A Y_____
2. motor		pike	_____
3. over		way	_____
4. motor		bike	_____
5. turn		cycle	_____

READING PRACTICE

1. Which underlined word is incorrect? Circle the letter.

> **GRAMMAR TO KNOW:**
> conditional sentences   infinitives
> prepositions   conjunctions

1. A <u>fast</u> way <u>getting</u> across town and avoid local traffic <u>is</u> on the freeway.
    A   Ⓑ   C

2. When <u>entering</u> the turnpike, be sure <u>to</u> yield <u>of</u> oncoming traffic.
           A   B   C

3. If you <u>didn't</u> want <u>to startle</u> a motorcycle driver, <u>pass</u> him slowly.
        A   B   C

4. There was a circle <u>at</u> the intersection of these two routes, <u>or</u> now there
                  A   B
   <u>is</u> an overpass.
   C

5. If you <u>feel</u> tired while <u>driving</u> on the turnpike, <u>pulled</u> into a rest stop.
        A   B   C

6. Trucks and trailers should stay <u>of</u> one side <u>of</u> the tollbooth while cars and
                              A   B
   vans <u>stay</u> on the other.
      C

7. Take the throughway <u>to</u> the beltway <u>while</u> then get off <u>at</u> Exit 7.
                 A   B   C

8. You will <u>paid</u> a large fine if you are caught <u>speeding</u> <u>on</u> the highway.
        A   B   C

9. It <u>is</u> extremely dangerous <u>drove</u> over the median <u>of</u> a highway.
     A   B   C

10. <u>To get</u> on the parkway, you must <u>merged</u> with the cars <u>on</u> the parkway.
    A   B   C

2. Read the following conversation and answer the questions.

Driver:	How do I get to the National Park?
Toll booth attendant:	Stay on the turnpike until Exit 15. That's the beltway around Philadelphia. Stay on the beltway until Exit 5A. Keep in the right hand lane because the exit is very close. The Park is at the exit.
Driver:	Do I pay the toll now?
Toll booth attendant:	No, pay when you get off the turnpike.
Driver:	What's the speed limit on the turnpike?
Toll booth attendant:	The same as any highway -- 55 m.p.h.

1. Where is the driver going?
    (A) To Philadelphia
    (B) To the National Park
    (C) To the toll booth

2. What is the driver's first exit?
    (A) Exit 15
    (B) Exit 5A
    (C) Exit 51

3. What highway circles Philadelphia?
    (A) The turnpike
    (B) The beltway
    (C) The parkway

4. What is the speed limit on the turnpike?
    (A) Less than the beltway
    (B) More than the freeway
    (C) The same as any highway

3. Read the following paragraph and answer the questions.

> The highway system makes it possible to cover hundreds of miles in a day. The speed limit is high, and rest stops along the road allow drivers to leave the highway and stop and eat. Once they have rested, drivers can easily and quickly get back on the highway.

1. How many miles can a person drive in one day on a highway?
    (A) Hundreds
    (B) Thousands
    (C) Dozens

2. Where can drivers stop and eat quickly?
    (A) At expensive restaurants
    (B) At rest stops
    (C) At toll booths

3. The speed limit on highways is
    (A) low
    (B) high
    (C) excessive

4. How much time do most drivers spend at a rest stop?
    (A) A short while
    (B) Several days
    (C) One week

UNIT ACTIVITIES

START TALKING

1. Pack your bag. (Class)

Name an item you will take on a trip. Your classmates will repeat the items already named and add one more item. If someone forgets an item, s/he is OUT; the game continues. Variation: Pack for a specific place.

Student 1:	I'm going on a trip, and I'll pack my jeans.
Student 2:	I'm going on a trip, and I'll pack my jeans and my blue shirt.

2. How do you get there? (Class)

Give a destination. Your classmates will tell you what transportation to use.

Student 1:	I need to go shopping.	Student 3:	Take a plane.
Student 2:	Take the bus.		I need to go home.
	I need to go to Paris.	Student 4:	Take your car.

PUT IT IN WRITING

1. Write down all the advantages and disadvantages of travel by train bus, plane, or car. Do your classmates agree with you?

2. Write a story about what is happening in this picture. First describe the room; then describe the actions. Share your story with the class.

Act It Out 1

Functions
Stating your wishes
Talking about yourself
Expressing excitement
Expressing desire
Planning a trip

Characters
A winner
Three friends

Setting
Four people in a room - one is just opening a letter.

Winner:	I won! I won! I won!
Friend 1:	Who? What? What did you win?
Winner:	A TRIP! A FREE trip! A free trip for TWO!
Friend 1:	Wow! Where?
Winner:	Anywhere! Where shall we go?
Friend 1:	We can drive to Chicago.
Winner:	Drive? Ourselves? This is a FREE trip.
Friend 1:	We can take a train to Chicago.
Winner:	Why Chicago? Think BIG! Let's go to Hong Kong.
Friend 1:	Great idea! We can take a boat to Hong Kong.

Winner:	Not me. I get sea sick.
Friend 1:	Well, I can't fly. I'm afraid to fly.
Winner:	No problem. I'll take someone else.
Friend 2:	I love to fly. Where are we going?
Winner:	Anywhere. I just won a free trip.
Friend 2:	I'll pack my bag and be right back.
Friend 1:	Hey. She invited me first.
Winner:	You don't like to fly.
Friend 2:	He doesn't like to do anything. Me, I love to do everything!
Winner:	Well, let's go to Africa.
Friend 2:	Africa? Too far.
Winner:	How about Nepal?
Friend 2:	Nepal? Too high.
Winner:	How about the Gobi Desert?
Friend 2:	The Gobi Desert? Too dry.
Winner:	You said you loved doing anything!
Friend 2:	I do. Unless it's too far, too high, or too dry.
Winner:	Forget it. I'll go by myself.

Act It Out 2

Do the skit again with new destinations.

Warm Up

We can take a _____ to _____.

train	Paris
bus	Tokyo
plane	Seoul
car	Singapore
boat	Berlin

Not me. I get _____.

air sick
car sick
sea sick
motion sickness.

IN BUSINESS

How many words from this unit can you identify. Write the words on the lines. Draw lines from the picture to the words.

19 TYPES OF BUSINESSES

WORDS TO KNOW

art gallery	customer	grocery store	record store
barbershop	department store	hair salon	restaurant
beauty parlor	dress store	jewelry store	shoe store
bicycle shop	drug store	luggage store	shopping mall
candy store	fast food place	office supply store	sporting goods store
clothing store	furniture store	pharmacy	toy store

WORD PRACTICE

1. Cross out the word that does NOT belong.

BUSINESS	RELATED PRODUCT OR SERVICE		
1. restaurant	menu	waiter	~~football~~
2. office supply store	staples	pens	bananas
3. jewelry store	shoes	bracelets	rings
4. clothing store	pants	lumber	dresses
5. pharmacy	aspirin	drugs	motor oil
6. barbershop	scissors	shave	boats
7. art gallery	cushions	frames	paintings
8. furniture store	beds	lamps	stationery
9. grocery store	computers	fruit	produce
10. sporting goods store	baseball	golf club	rubber bands

2. Who works at these places? Circle the correct profession.

WORK PLACE	PROFESSION	
1. restaurant	(chef)	diner
2. jewelry store	jeweler	thief
3. hair salon	hair stylist	bartender
4. grocery store	gardener	grocer
5. pharmacy	farmer	pharmacist

3. Circle the correct word.

1. I need a new pair of shoes.
   I should go to the ((shoe store) / grocery store).

2. I need a new suitcase.
   I should go to the (clothing store / luggage store).

3. I need a new hat.
   I should go to the (hair salon / department store).

4. I need some medicine.
   I should go to the (drug store / record store).

5. I want a new record and a compact disc.
   I should go to the (record store / office supply store).

4. Look at the map of the shopping mall. Answer the questions below.

		Restaurant	Shoe Store	Toy Store	Furniture Store	Dress Shop
Department Store						
		Candy Store	Hair Salon	Drug Store	Bike Shop	Art Gallery

1. Can I buy some shoes at the mall? _YES, YOU CAN._
   Where? _AT THE SHOE STORE. BETWEEN THE RESTAURANT AND THE TOY STORE._

2. Can I buy a toy for my niece? _____
   Where? _____
   _____

3. Can I get my hair cut? _____
   Where? _____
   _____

4. Can I buy a new bike? _____
   Where? _____
   _____

5. Can I look at some bedroom furniture? _____
   Where? _____
   _____

5. Draw a line between the business and a product available at the business.

BUSINESS	PRODUCT
1. toy store	sandals
2. record store	prescription medicine
3. candy store	overnight bags
4. bicycle shop	dolls
5. pharmacy	compact discs
6. shoe store	racing bikes
7. luggage store	chocolate bars

READING PRACTICE

1. Which underlined word is incorrect?   Circle the letter.

> **GRAMMAR TO KNOW:**
> articles   prepositions
> subject-verb agreement   gerunds

1. The art gallery will get more visitors <u>by</u> <u>open</u> <u>on</u> Sundays.
      A Ⓑ C

2. Today I must <u>go</u> <u>at</u> the pharmacy, the hair salon <u>and</u> the grocery store.
    A B   C

3. I prefer the small cafe <u>on</u> Main Street because <u>the</u> restaurant <u>are</u> noisy.
          A   B   C

4. My son just <u>got</u> a job <u>of</u> the record store <u>in</u> the shopping mall.
       A   B   C

5. Barbara always enjoys <u>to shop</u> <u>in</u> small dress stores <u>rather</u> than large
              A   B   C
department stores.

6. <u>The</u> new luggage store <u>is doing</u> a lot of <u>the</u> business already.
  A   B   C

7. Candy stores, fast food places <u>and</u> bicycle shops <u>are</u> a few places where
                 A   B
young teenagers <u>goes</u>.
       C

8. Because the barbershop gave <u>the</u> less expensive haircuts, <u>it</u> <u>put</u> the hair
                 A   B C
salon out of business.

9. <u>The</u> beautiful windows <u>of</u> the new jewelry store <u>attracts</u> many customers.
  A   B   C

10. Surprised that <u>the</u> office supply store didn't <u>have</u> office chairs, the man
          A   B
went <u>of</u> the furniture store.
     C

2. Read the following passage and answer the questions.

> The shopping mall has four floors of shops. There are many small specialty shops selling imported shoes and clothes, and two large department stores which sell everything. On the first level are ten fast food places selling food from all parts of the world.

1. What is the passage about?
   - (A) Import taxes
   - (B) Shoe styles
   - (C) A shopping mall

2. How many floors are there?
   - (A) One
   - (B) Two
   - (C) Four

3. What's on the first level?
   - (A) Fast food places
   - (B) Imported shoes
   - (C) Department stores

4. Where is the food from?
   - (A) The neighborhood
   - (B) The suburbs
   - (C) All over the world

3. Read the following conversation and answer the questions:

> Bob: Can you tell me where the shoe store is?
> Mary: Yes, it's on Main Street between the hair salon and the record store.
> Bob: Is it across from the jewelry store?
> Mary: No, it's across from the pharmacy.

1. Where is the shoe store?
   - (A) By the jewelry store
   - (B) Across from the record store
   - (C) Next to the hair salon

2. Which is NOT on Main Street?
   - (A) Hair salon
   - (B) Shoe store
   - (C) Police station

3. Where is the record store?
   - (A) Next to the shoe store
   - (B) Across from the jewelry store
   - (C) Next to the pharmacy

4. Where is the pharmacy?
   - (A) Across from the shoe store
   - (B) Next to the jewelry store
   - (C) Next to the hair salon

20 OFFICE TERMS

WORDS TO KNOW

bookcase	document	manager	receptionist
boss	drawer	mistake	rolodex
calendar	envelope	out-box	secretary
client	file	outside line	supplies
correction	file cabinet	paper clip	telephone
desk	in-box	photocopy	wastebasket

WORD PRACTICE

1. Complete the following sentences.

1. Mail to be read is in my <u>I N - B O X</u> .

2. Mail that is read and is to be filed is in my <u>O</u> __ __ - __ __ __ .

3. Important business papers are filed by the clerical worker in a

   <u>F</u> __ __ __   <u>C</u> __ __ __ __ <u>E T</u>.

4. Put the letter in a large <u>E</u> __ __ __ __ __ __ __ and stamp it.

5. Dial 9 for an <u>O</u> __ __ <u>S</u> __ __ __ <u>L</u> __ __ __.

6. Each worker sits at his own <u>D</u> __ __ __.

7. The <u>C L</u> __ __ __ __ __ __ workers must file all the correspondence.

8. The office <u>M</u> __ __ __ __ __ <u>R</u> sent a memo to all the typists.

2. Draw a line between words that are associated with one another.

boss	desk
file	correction
mistake	out-box
envelope	file cabinet
drawer	employee
in-box	letter

3. Cross out the word that does NOT belong.

1. desk   ~~pencil~~   bookcase
2. envelope   client   letter
3. manager   receptionist   pen
4. calendar   boss   secretary
5. paper clip   telephone   staple

4. Circle the supplies you might find in a desk drawer. (5 words)

file cabinet	mistake	pen	bookcase
(envelope)	paper	pencil	telephone
paper clip	typist	waste paper	receptionist

5. Fill in the blanks.

The _R E C E P T I O N I S T_ is an important person in an office. She answers the _T_ _ _ _ _ _ _ _ _ _E_, takes _M_ _ _ _ _ _ _ _S_ for the _B_ _ _ _S_ and greets visitors. Sometimes she also sorts the mail.

6. Draw a line between the noun and the corresponding activity.

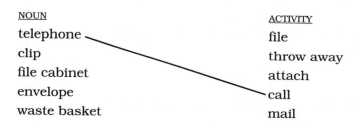

NOUN

telephone
clip
file cabinet
envelope
waste basket

ACTIVITY

file
throw away
attach
call
mail

7. Write the words for the objects below.

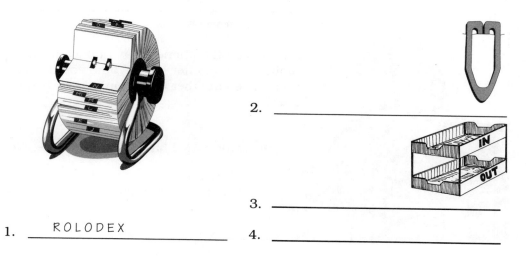

1. ___ROLODEX___

2. _____

3. _____

4. _____

READING PRACTICE

1. Which underlined word is incorrect? Circle the letter.

> **GRAMMAR TO KNOW:**
> conditional sentences   conjunctions
> subject-verb agreement   prepositions

1. The secretary put a paper clip <u>of</u> the loose papers and <u>returned</u> them <u>to</u>
                             (A)   B   C
   their file in the file cabinet.

2. <u>My</u> secretary <u>use</u> a word processor rather <u>than</u> a typewriter.
    A   B   C

3. I <u>has</u> a <u>10 o'clock</u> appointment <u>with</u> my boss.
     A   B   C

4. When the receptionist <u>goes</u> <u>to</u> lunch, you should <u>answered</u> the phone.
                     A B   C

5. Please <u>put</u> the envelope <u>at</u> <u>my</u> in-box.
          A   B C

6. The secretary <u>sat</u> at his desk <u>or</u> opened the <u>mail</u>.
          A   B   C

7. The manager <u>order</u> some supplies: pens, a <u>rolodex</u> <u>and</u> paper clips.
           A   B   C

8. The phone number <u>was</u> among my messages, <u>which</u> were thrown <u>on</u>
                  A   B   C
   the wastepaper basket.

9. If the new manager <u>arrives</u> <u>on</u> Tuesday, we can <u>started</u>
                  A B   C
   our project.

10. Ask <u>the</u> receptionist to <u>gives</u> you <u>an</u> outside line.
        A   B   C

TELEPHONE EXPRESSIONS

Mr. Smith is on the phone. May I take a message?
Mr. Smith is on another line. Would you like to hold?
Mr. Smith is on another call. Could he return your call later?

Operator, may I have an outside line, please?

The number you dialed is no longer in service.   Please hang up and try again.

2. Read the following conversation and answer the questions.

> Boss: Do you have the letter we received yesterday from the Smith Company?
>
> Secretary: Yes, I filed it already. Do you want to see it?
>
> Boss: Yes, I want to re-read it before I reply.
>
> Secretary: Here it is. Let me photocopy it for you.

1. Who is the letter from?
   (A) The boss
   (B) The Smith Company
   (C) The secretary

2. The boss wants to see the letter before
   (A) he replies to it
   (B) it is thrown away
   (C) the secretary mails it

3. Where did the secretary put the letter?
   (A) In the in-box
   (B) In a file folder
   (C) In the mail

4. What will the secretary do with the letter?
   (A) Mail it
   (B) Fold it
   (C) Photocopy it

3. Read the following paragraph and answer the questions.

> Twenty years ago, the photocopy machine was a convenience. Today, it's a necessity for the efficient office. Photocopies of documents are exact reproductions of the original documents. They can be made quickly and cheaply.

1. When were photocopiers merely a convenience?
   (A) 15 years ago
   (B) 20 years ago
   (C) 25 years ago

2. Today the photocopy machine is an office
   (A) luxury
   (B) necessity
   (C) benefit

3. What are photocopies?
   (A) Souvenir snapshots
   (B) Carbon papers
   (C) Exact reproductions

4. How can photocopies be made?
   (A) Slowly but surely
   (B) Quickly and cheaply
   (C) Expensively and poorly

PHOTOCOPY EXPRESSIONS

1. Make 4 copies for me.

2. Copy this back-to-back. = Use both sides of the paper.

21 | OFFICE EQUIPMENT

WORDS TO KNOW

answering machine	fax (facsimile)	operator	typewriter
calculator	fax machine	photocopier	typist
computer	floppy disk	printer	typo
courier	memorandum	stapler	voicemail
diskette	message	telephone	word processor

WORD PRACTICE

1. Write the noun form for each of the following verbs.

1. compute   _COMPUTER_____

2. operate   _____

3. type   _____

4. photocopy   _____

5. staple   _____

6. calculate   _____

2. Write the words for machines used in an office.

1. A _T E L E P H O N E_ is used to call clients.

2. A _C_ __ __ _C_ __ __ __ __ __ __ is used to add numbers.

3. A _C_ __ __ _P_ __ __ __ _R_ is used to maintain records.

4. A _S_ __ __ _P_ __ __ _R_ is used to attach papers together.

5. A _P_ __ __ _T_ __ __ __ __ __ __ __ is used to make copies.

6. A _W_ __ __ _D_   _P_ __ __ __ __ __ __ __ _R_ is used

to prepare documents.

7. _V_ __ __ _C_ __ __ __ __ __ answers your telephone and takes your

messages electronically.

3. Write the word under the appropriate label.

	MACHINES	PEOPLE
fax machine	*FAX MACHINE*	
boss		*BOSS*
answering machine		
secretary		
computer		
typist		
employee		
client		
telephone		
word processor		
photocopier		

4. Draw a line between the word and its abbreviation.

WORD	ABBREVIATION
typographical error	memo
facsimile	phone
photocopy	typo
memorandum	fax
telephone	copy

5. Write these words under the appropriate label.

memorandum   electric typewriter   word processor   by hand   (2)
mail   fax   (2)   letter   courier

TYPES OF BUSINESS CORRESPONDENCE

MEMORANDUM

_____

_____

WAYS TO PREPARE CORRESPONDENCE

_____

_____

_____

WAYS TO SEND CORRESPONDENCE

_____

_____

_____

_____

6. Cross out the word that does NOT belong.

1. envelope   ~~floppy disk~~   letter   paper
2. pencil   typewriter   computer   photocopier
3. boss   photocopy   typist   secretary
4. fax   mail   telephone   drawer
5. desk   office   mistakes   filing cabinet

READING PRACTICE

1. Which underlined word is incorrect? Circle the letter.

> **GRAMMAR TO KNOW:**
> infinitives   prepositions
> subject-verb agreement   verb·tense

1. Please <u>stores</u> all <u>of</u> your files <u>on</u> this diskette, not on a floppy disk.
   (A)   B   C

2. When the paper <u>becomes</u> jammed <u>in</u> the printer, the secretary went <u>to tell</u>
   A   B   C

   the boss.

3. This <u>is</u> our new employee. Will you <u>show</u> him how <u>sending</u> a fax?
   A   B   C

4. If the typist <u>make</u> a mistake <u>on</u> the word processor, he can <u>fix</u> it easily.
   A   B   C

5. The courier picked <u>up</u> the <u>mail</u> for the office <u>to</u> West Street.
   A   B   C

6. A secretary <u>answered</u> the <u>phone</u>, types letters, <u>and</u> sends memoranda.
   A   B   C

7. <u>Was</u> there <u>a</u> message <u>of</u> Miss Collins in your voicemail?
   A   B   C

8. The fax is <u>at</u> a folder <u>on</u> top <u>of</u> the filing cabinet.
   A   B   C

9. <u>Every</u> week, Mr. Suarez <u>using</u> his calculator <u>to</u> calculate his pay.
   A   B   C

10. Since <u>the</u> voicemail message had <u>no</u> phone number, there was no way
    A   B

    <u>returning</u> the call.
    C

2. Read the following paragraph and answer the questions.

> Miss Cordell is a typist. She works in a small office. She types letters and mails them. Before she sends a letter, she makes a photocopy and puts the copy in the files.

1. What is Miss Cordell's profession?
    (A) Mail carrier
    (B) Typist
    (C) Office manager

2. Where does Miss Cordell work?
    (A) A store
    (B) An office
    (C) A school

3. Miss Cordell makes a photocopy after she
    (A) types a letter
    (B) mails a letter
    (C) files a letter

4. What does Miss Cordell put in the files?
    (A) A copy of the letter
    (B) A pencil
    (C) The mail

3. Read the following conversation and answer the questions.

> Boss: Did you finish typing the fax?
> Secretary: Yes. Do you want it to be sent today?
> Boss: As soon as possible. Can you do it now?
> Secretary: I'm just filing letters, so I'll do the filing later, and I'll send out the fax right away.
> Boss: Great. Our client will have it when he gets back from lunch.

1. When should the fax be sent?
    (A) This morning
    (B) Immediately
    (C) After lunch

2. What is the typist doing now?
    (A) Sending the fax
    (B) Typing the fax
    (C) Filing letters

3. Who is sending the fax?
    (A) The client
    (B) A restaurant chef
    (C) The secretary

4. Who will receive the fax?
    (A) A client
    (B) A chef
    (C) The mailman

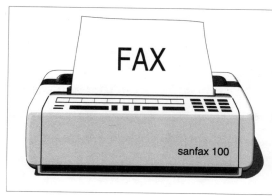

FAX EXPRESSIONS

1. I received a fax.
2. I sent a fax.

3. I faxed a letter to him.
4. Fax me your proposal.
5. She'll fax it to me later.

6. What is your fax number?

22 CONSTRUCTION

WORDS TO KNOW

bathtub	fixture	outlets	saw
board	foreman	paint	screw
burned out	fuse	painter	screwdriver
carpenter	glue	pipe	switch
connect	hammer	plaster	tool
contractor	handyman	plug	toolbox
current	homeowner	plumber	turn on/off
drain	inch	plunger	washer
drill	leak	power	wire
drip	measure	ruler	wood
electrician	metal	running water	woodwork
faucet	meter	sand	work bench
file	nail	sandpaper	wrench

WORD PRACTICE

1. Draw a line between associated words.

VERB
to hammer
to measure
to cut
to drain
to screw
to sand
to turn on

NOUN
sand paper
nail
power
screwdriver
ruler
saw
sink

2. Fill in the blanks.

A Carpenter

A carpenter keeps his _T O O L S_ in a _T _ _ _ B _ _._
He carries a _S _ __ , a _H _ _ M _ _ __ , a _D _ _ _ _ _ , and a
_F _ L __ in it. He also has lots of _N _ _ _ _ S_ in the toolbox, and
_S _ _ E _ __ as well. There is also a _R _ _ _ R_ because he is
careful to _M _ _ _ _ _ _ _ each piece of _W _ _ __ before he
_C _ _ __ it.

3. Complete these sentences by adding *-ing* to the words in parentheses.

> **NOTE THESE DIFFERENCES:**
> drip   dripping
> plug   plugging

1. The carpenter is (saw) _____*SAWING*_____ a piece of wood into two pieces.

2. The handyman is (hammer) _____ a nail into the wall.

3. The foreman is (drill) _____ a hole for a screw.

4. The painter is (sand) _____ the wood to make it smooth.

5. The plumber is (drain) _____ the water from the sink.

6. The water is (leak) _____ from the faucet.

7. The faucet is (drip) _____ water.

8. The electrician is (plug) _____ the lamp into the outlet.

9. The contractor is (turn on) _____ the power to the house.

10. The homeowner is (look for) _____ a burned-out fuse.

4. Cross out the word that does NOT belong.

1. nail   ~~ruler~~   screw
2. leak   saw   board
3. fuse   sandpaper   file
4. board   screwdriver   wood
5. switch   turn on   sink
6. measure   light   lamp
7. turn off   power   work bench
8. current   meter   window
9. wire   faucet   running water
10. bathtub   saw   shower

5. Draw a line to create a new compound noun. Write the new compound noun.

NOUN	+	NOUN	COMPOUND NOUN
bath		driver	*BATHTUB*
sand		bench	_____
tool		tub	_____
work		paper	_____
screw		box	_____

6. Fill in the blanks.

A Plumber

Sometimes water does not drain from a sink. If a <u>S</u> <u>I</u> <u>N</u> <u>K</u> doesn't drain, something may be plugging the <u>D</u> <u>R</u> __ __ __ . If the drain is stopped up, the <u>P</u> __ __ <u>M</u> __ __ __ may use a tool called a <u>P</u> __ __ <u>N</u> __ __ __ to clear the <u>P</u> __ __ __ <u>S</u> .

READING PRACTICE

1. Which underlined word is incorrect? Circle the letter.

> **GRAMMAR TO KNOW:**
> conditional sentences   gerunds
> prepositions   verb tense

1. Please <u>use</u> sandpaper <u>in</u> the woodwork to make <u>it</u> smooth.
   A   Ⓑ   C

2. The plywood <u>that</u> the carpenter <u>use</u> was not thick enough <u>for</u> the wall.
            A   B   C

3. <u>Worked</u> quickly, the electrician <u>connected</u> the wall fixtures <u>safely</u> to the
   A   B   C
   outlets.

4. There <u>is</u> a problem <u>for</u> the electrical outlets <u>in</u> this house.
         A   B   C

5. If <u>the</u> toilet <u>would</u> not <u>flush</u>, the plumber uses a plunger.
     A   B   C

6. Katherine opened the plug, <u>let</u> the water <u>drain</u> out <u>of</u> the sink.
                            A   B   C

7. The plumber will <u>came</u> tomorrow <u>to fix</u> the <u>leaking</u> pipe in the kitchen.
                 A   B   C

8. If you <u>leave</u> the house, you <u>should</u> always <u>turned</u> off the lights.
           A   B   C

9. The electrician came <u>to</u> our house and <u>fix</u> <u>the</u> wires yesterday.
                       A   B C

10. Today the carpenters <u>will</u> install the glass <u>at</u> all <u>of</u> the windows.
                    A   B   C

A hardhat must be worn at all construction sites.

Construction workers are often called "hardhats".

2. Read the following paragraph and answer the questions.

> Some electrical problems can be easily fixed. When a lightbulb burns out, a whole room can go dark. You can easily replace a light bulb yourself. When a fuse burns out, a whole house can go dark. You can easily replace a fuse, too. You can do small wiring jobs at home. Large wiring jobs should be done by an electrician.

1. What is an example of an easy electrical problem?
    (A) An electrical fire
    (B) A burned-out bulb
    (C) Complicated wiring

2. What can return electric power to a house?
    (A) A telephone call
    (B) A new fuse
    (C) Solar power

3. Who should be called for large wiring jobs?
    (A) A plumber
    (B) A carpenter
    (C) An electrician

4. This passage discusses electricity
    (A) on the job
    (B) at home
    (C) at night

3. Read the following conversation and answer the questions.

> Plumber: Hello. ABC Plumbing.
> Customer: Hello. I need a plumber.
> Plumber: What's the problem?
> Customer: A dripping faucet. It's been dripping for a week. It won't stop dripping.
> Plumber: OK. We'll be there tomorrow morning.

1. Where does this conversation take place?
    (A) On the telephone
    (B) In a plumbing supply shop
    (C) At the front door

2. What is the name of the plumbing company?
    (A) OK Plumbing
    (B) Hello Plumbing
    (C) ABC Plumbing

3. What is the problem?
    (A) No hot water
    (B) A dripping faucet
    (C) A leaky bathtub

4. When will the plumber come?
    (A) Right away
    (B) Next week
    (C) Tomorrow

Question: How many English teachers does it take to screw in a lightbulb?

Answer: Three. One to hold the bulb. One to hold the ladder. And one to read the directions.

23 MEDICINE

WORDS TO KNOW

ache	disease	infection	physician
ambulance	doctor	injection	pill
aspirin	drill	injury	prescription
bandage	emergency	medication	sick
bone	fever	medicine	sore
broken	headache	nurse	temperature
clinic	heal	operation	tooth / teeth
cold	hurt	pain	toothache
cure	ill	patient	treatment
dentist	illness	pharmacist	x-ray

WORD PRACTICE

1. Draw a line between words with similar meanings.

fever   ill
hurt   disease
medication   doctor
physician   medicine
sick   ache
illness   temperature

2. Complete the sentences.

1. A <u>N</u> <u>U</u> <u>R</u> <u>S</u> <u>E</u> works in a hospital.

2. A tooth problem is treated by a <u>D</u> _ _ _ _ _ <u>T</u> .

3. A doctor takes care of <u>P</u> _ _ _ _ _ _ _ _ .

4. A <u>B</u> _ _ _ _ _ bone will heal.

5. A pharmacist fills a <u>P</u> _ _ _ _ _ _ _ _ _ _ _ _ .

3. Write the noun forms of the verbs below.

VERB	NOUN	VERB	NOUN
1. prescribe	_PRESCRIPTION_	4. injure	_____
2. medicate	_____	5. treat	_____
3. operate	_____	6. infect	_____

4. Write the words associated with doctors or dentists under the labels. Some words are used twice.

a cold   drill   headache   toothache
x–ray   broken   tooth   infection

DOCTORS   DENTISTS

_A COLD_____   _DRILL_____

_____   _____

_____   _____

_____   _____

_____   _____

_____   _____

5. Cross out the word that does NOT belong.

1. sick   ~~bandage~~   ill
2. doctor   physician   operation
3. a cold   medication   prescription
4. ambulance   dentist   toothache
5. broken   treat   cure
6. aspirin   medicine   x–ray
7. clinic   bone   hospital

6. Fill in the blanks.

In the Hospital

When a _P_ _A_ _T_ _I_ _E_ _N_ _T_ is in the _H_ _O_ _ _ _ _ _ _ ,
he usually stays in bed. The _N_ _ _ _R_ _ _ _ brings him what he needs.
She brings _M_ _ _ _ _ _A_ _ _ _ _ and _P_ _ _ _L_ _S_ and
gives _I_ _N_ _ _ _ _ _ _ _ _ . If the patient needs an _X_ - _ _ _ or
an _O_ _ _ _R_ _ _ _ _ _ , she helps him prepare for it. Usually
the _D_ _ _ _ _ _ _R_ will come in once a day for a short visit.

A nurse's cap can tell us where the nurse went to school. Each nursing school has its own cap.

7. Write the word under the appropriate category.

	PERSON	CONDITION	THING
prescription	_____	_____	*PRESCRIPTION*
ache	_____	*ACHE*	_____
bandage	_____	_____	_____
dentist	*DENTIST*	_____	_____
fever	_____	_____	_____
headache	_____	_____	_____
infection	_____	_____	_____
medicine	_____	_____	_____
nurse	_____	_____	_____
patient	_____	_____	_____
sore	_____	_____	_____
drill	_____	_____	_____

READING PRACTICE

1. Which underlined word is incorrect? Circle the letter.

> **GRAMMAR TO KNOW:**
> conjunctions   infinitives
> prepositions   verb tense

1. This patient <u>is</u> very sick <u>or</u> should be <u>taken</u> to the hospital immediately.
      A   Ⓑ   C

2. Are you <u>under</u> <u>a</u> physician's order <u>taking</u> that medication?
        A B   C

3. There <u>is</u> a cure <u>at</u> this disease, but <u>the</u> drugs are very expensive.
      A   B   C

4. The medics <u>in</u> the ambulance were able <u>saving</u> the patient's life before
          A   B
   they arrived <u>at</u> the emergency room.
         C

5. The doctor <u>removing</u> the bandages to <u>see</u> if the infection had <u>healed</u>.
        A   B   C

6. Because <u>the</u> patient was <u>in</u> pain, the nurse <u>gives</u> her medication.
        A   B   C

7. A fever <u>also</u> a headache could <u>be</u> signs of <u>a</u> more serious illness.
       A   B   C

8. The dentist drilled <u>through</u> the tooth to get <u>of</u> the source <u>of</u> the pain.
          A   B   C

9. If you <u>stayed</u> in bed <u>for</u> a few days, the soreness will <u>disappear</u>.
      A   B   C

10. The x–ray revealed that Sally <u>has</u> a <u>broken</u> bone <u>of</u> her foot.
          A   B   C

2. Read the following conversation and answer the questions.

Doctor:	What seems to be the problem?
Patient:	I have a fever. My temperature is over 102 degrees.
Doctor:	You seem to have an infection in the cut on your hand.
Patient:	Yes. I cut myself yesterday with a knife.
Doctor:	Take this prescription to the drugstore. This medicine will cure the infection.

1. What is the patient's problem?
   (A) A cold
   (B) An infection
   (C) A broken bone

3. How did the patient hurt himself?
   (A) With a bat
   (B) With a pencil
   (C) With a knife

2. Where is the patient's infection?
   (A) On the hand
   (B) On the face
   (C) On the feet

4. Where will the prescription be filled?
   (A) At the drugstore
   (B) At the doctor's office
   (C) In the kitchen

3. Read the following passage and answer the questions.

> Mr. Jones had an operation yesterday. He is not in pain now, because the nurse has given him an injection. He also has taken some pills to help him relax. He can see a bandage on his stomach. Mr. Jones is glad the operation is finished.

1. Mr. Jones is probably in a
   (A) cafeteria
   (B) car
   (C) hospital

3. What helps Mr. Jones relax?
   (A) The operation
   (B) Some medication
   (C) The doctor

2. Where was Mr. Jones's problem?
   (A) In his stomach
   (B) On his back
   (C) In his leg

4. How does Mr. Jones feel about the operation?
   (A) He wants to do it again.
   (B) He is still afraid.
   (C) He is glad it is over.

MEDICAL SYMBOL

This is the international symbol of the medical profession: Two serpents entwined around a winged staff.

24 THE MILITARY

WORDS TO KNOW

airfield	duty	off-duty	serve
Air Force	enlist	on-duty	service
Army	fly	officer	soldier
barracks	infantry	parade	stripe
base	inspection	pilot	submarine
camp	march	rank	tank
Coast Guard	Marines	recruit	tour
combat	mess hall	reserves	troops
draft	military	rifle	uniform
drill	Navy	sailor	veteran

WORD PRACTICE

1. Write the words that are defined below.

    1. to walk in military formation: <u>M</u> <u>A</u> <u>R</u> <u>C</u> <u>H</u>

    2. where soldiers sleep: <u>B</u> __ __ __ __ __ __ <u>S</u>

    3. underwater ship: <u>S</u> __ __ <u>M</u> <u>A</u> <u>R</u> __ __ <u>E</u>

    4. a soldier's clothing: <u>U</u> __ __ __ __ __ <u>M</u>

    5. groups of soldiers: <u>T</u> __ __ __ <u>P</u> <u>S</u>

    6. military practice: <u>D</u> __ __ __ <u>L</u>

2. Idiom practice: fill in the blanks with words from the list above.

    1. A military person is " in the <u>S</u> <u>E</u> <u>R</u> <u>V</u> <u>I</u> <u>C</u> <u>E</u> ."

    2. A soldier at work is " on <u>D</u> __ __ <u>Y</u> ."

    3. A military person in official clothes is " in <u>U</u> __ __ <u>F</u> __ __ <u>M</u> ."

    4. A soldier away from the army camp is " off <u>B</u> __ __ <u>E</u> ."

    5. Soldiers fighting are "in <u>C</u> __ __ <u>B</u> __ <u>T</u> ."

3. Write the *-ing* form of these verbs to complete these sentences.

VERBS   SENTENCES

1. fly   The pilots are _____*FLYING*_____ the jets.

2. drill   The new recruits are tired of _____ .

3. enlist   The students are thinking about _____ in

      the Army.

4. inspect The sergeant is _____ the barracks.

5. sail   The ship is _____ this evening.

6. march The soldiers are _____ on the field.

7. recruit The officers are _____ pilots for the Air Force.

8. join   The woman is _____ the Army.

4. Draw a line between military words and their general meanings.

mess hall   practice

drill   dormitory

base   clothes

uniform   fighting

combat   "town"

barracks   dining room

5. Write the word under the appropriate category.

	PERSON	TYPE OF TRANSPORTATION	PLACE
veteran	*VETERAN*		
submarine		*SUBMARINE*	
soldier			
officer			
mess hall			*MESS HALL*
camp			
tank			
barracks			

READING PRACTICE

1. Which underlined word is incorrect? Circle the letter.

> **GRAMMAR TO KNOW:**
> modal auxiliaries   conjunctions
> subject-verb agreement prepositions

1. My uncle <u>was recruited</u> <u>in</u> the Army <u>and</u> served a 15-year military career.
           A   Ⓑ   C

2. <u>In</u> the Navy most sailors <u>are expected</u> to serve <u>at</u> a submarine.
  A   B   C

3. <u>Most</u> personnel who enlist <u>in</u> the Air Force <u>will</u> like to fly jets.
   A   B   C

4. The troops <u>marched</u> past the mess hall <u>while</u> returned <u>to</u> the barracks.
         A   B   C

5. Veterans <u>but</u> reserve officers, <u>as well as</u> troops in uniform, <u>marched</u>
         A   B   C
   in today's parade.

6. Soldiers <u>must</u> <u>drill</u> for combat with rifles <u>also</u> tanks.
        A B   C

7. <u>The</u> third infantry <u>hope</u> to pass <u>inspection</u> this morning.
  A   B   C

8. Whether they <u>are</u> on-duty or off-duty, the soldiers must <u>been</u> <u>in</u> uniform.
          A   B C

9. To avoid <u>being</u> drafted <u>into</u> the Army, many men <u>enlists</u> in the Navy.
        A   B   C

10. The Air Force <u>practice</u> drills <u>on</u> the airfield <u>all</u> day.
          A   B   C

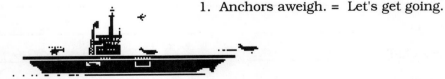

EVERYDAY EXPRESSIONS WITH MILITARY TERMS

1. Anchors aweigh. = Let's get going.

2. This place is like boot camp. =
   This place demands a lot of hard work.

3. SNAFU =
   Situation Normal; All Fouled Up.

---

2. Read the following paragraph and answer the questions.

> More than twenty years ago, all eighteen-year-old men regis-tered for military service. This registration was part of "the draft." If you were drafted, you were conscripted into the Army. About twenty years ago, this "draft" system was discontinued. Today the army is composed almost entirely of volunteers.

1. Today the army is made up of
   (A) draftees
   (B) volunteers
   (C) officers

2. When was the draft last used?
   (A) 8 years ago
   (B) About 20 years ago
   (C) 100 years ago

3. At what age did men register for the draft?
   (A) 18
   (B) 19
   (C) 20

4. Which of the following is true of the draft system?
   (A) It's no longer in use.
   (B) It's a volunteer organization.
   (C) It's only for men under 18.

3. Read the following conversation and answer the questions.

> Luke: Were you in the Army?
> Mark: Yes, I was drafted twenty years ago.
> Luke: I was in the Navy, but I enlisted.
> Mark: My brother was a sailor, too.
> Luke: Actually, I was a Navy pilot.

1. How did Mark join the Army?
   (A) He volunteered.
   (B) He signed up.
   (C) He was drafted.

2. What did Luke enlist in?
   (A) The Army
   (B) The Navy
   (C) The Air Force

3. Mark's brother was a
   (A) sailor
   (B) pilot
   (C) marine

4. What was Luke's job in the Navy?
   (A) Sailor
   (B) Pilot
   (C) Admiral

ASTRONAUTS

Separate from the Army, Navy, and Air Force is NASA, the National Aeronautic and Space Adminis-tration.

NASA operates the Space Shuttle and sends astro-nauts to outer space.

The word *astronauts* means "sailors of the stars."

25 THE POLICE AND THE LAW

WORDS TO KNOW

arrest	guard	police car	suspicion
attorney	handcuffs	policeman	testify
case	imprison	police officer	testimony
cell	jail	police station	thief
court	judge	policewoman	trial
crime	jury	prison	try
criminal	lawyer	prisoner	victim
defendant	misdemeanor	prosecutor	violate
defense	officer	robber	violator
felony	patrol	sentence	violation
fine	patrol car	suspect	witness

WORD PRACTICE

1. Draw a line between words that are similar in meaning.

policewoman   misdemeanor
violation   lawyer
jail   robber
patrol car   officer
thief   prison
attorney   police car

2. Write the noun for the *person*.

PLACE OR ACT		PERSON	
1. robbery	The	_ROBBER_	stole the camera.
2. crime	The	_____	was sent to jail.
3. prosecution	The	_____	won the case.
4. judgement	The	_____	sentenced the criminal.
5. theft	The	_____	picked my pocket.
6. prison	The	_____	waited in her cell.

POLICE OFFICER'S BADGE

This badge represents the authority of the police officer. It is used for identification. (The word "identification" is often shortened to ID. The badge is a police officer's ID.)

3. Past Tense Review: Add *-d* or *-ed* to the following verbs.

1. jail   _JAILED_____

2. sentence   _____

3. fine   _____

4. arrest   _____

5. imprison   _____

6. judge   _____

7. witness   _____

4. Write the Simple Present Tense of the verb in the sentences below.

1. A person _____ _TESTIFIES_____ under oath.
   (*testify*)

2. Someone always _____ a public crime.
   (*witness*)

3. A criminal _____ the law.
   (*violates*)

4. A judge _____ criminals who are guilty.
   (*sentence*)

5. A police officer _____ criminals.
   (*arrest*)

5. Write the noun form of the verb. Some may have two forms.

VERB	NOUN
1. to suspect	_SUSPECT / SUSPICION_____
2. to testify	_____
3. to violate	_____
4. to imprison	_____
5. to prosecute	_____
6. to defend	_____
7. to rob	_____

READING PRACTICE

1. Which underlined word is incorrect? Circle the letter.

> **GRAMMAR TO KNOW:**
> adjective comparisons   infinitives
> conditional sentences   two-word verbs

1. The suspect was arrested <u>and</u> charged <u>for</u> a crime he had <u>never</u>
                    A   (B)   C
   committed.

2. The policewoman <u>was off-duty</u> when she came <u>across</u> the <u>worse</u>
                     A   B   C
   accident she had ever seen.

3. The suspect can <u>had</u> a lawyer <u>represent</u> him if <u>he</u> wishes.
               A   B   C

4. The prosecutor <u>called</u> the witness <u>up</u> before the jury <u>testify</u>.
               A   B   C

5. <u>The</u> defendant was <u>brought out</u> her jail cell <u>into</u> the courtroom.
     A   B   C

6. Because Mr. Simon committed <u>a</u> felony, he had <u>wearing</u> handcuffs
                                A   B
   <u>to</u> his trial.
   C

7. The judge reviewed <u>the</u> case <u>and</u> pronounced <u>longest</u> jail sentence allowed
                    B   A   C
   by law.

8. The prisoner <u>attempted</u> <u>grab</u> the gun <u>from</u> the guard.
               A   B   C

9. <u>The</u> defense lawyer <u>went</u> to <u>look of</u> the important file.
     A   B   C

10. You <u>would</u> have to go <u>to</u> court if you refuse <u>to pay</u> your traffic ticket.
         A   B   C

JUDICIAL SYMBOL

This is the symbol of the law. It represents the balance between right and wrong.

2. Read the following conversation and answer the questions.

Man:	Officer! Officer! This woman robbed me! She's a thief!
Woman:	He's crazy. Arrest him. Put handcuffs on him. Put him in jail and throw away the key.
Man:	Don't listen to her. I want my attorney. She took my watch. I have witnesses. They'll testify at the trial.
Woman:	You left your watch at home, moron.
Officer:	Are you two husband and wife?
Woman:	Of course! Do you think I would talk to this man otherwise?
Man:	She's a liar. A convicted felon. Don't listen to her.

1. What did the man accuse the woman of?
   (A) Robbing him
   (B) Stealing a car
   (C) Selling his watch

2. What does the woman suggest the officer do to the man?
   (A) Give him a ride
   (B) Ask him his age
   (C) Put him in jail

3. Where did the man leave his watch?
   (A) At the police station
   (B) At home
   (C) At the trial

4. The man and woman are
   (A) lost
   (B) married
   (C) guilty

3. Read the following paragraph and answer the questions.

A judge presides over a court trial. The prosecuting attorney presents the case for the victim. The lawyer for the defense presents the case for the defendant. The jury listens to the arguments. The twelve people on the jury decide whether the defendant is guilty or not guilty.

If the defendant is guilty, he or she will be sentenced by the judge. The judge can fine the criminal (for example, a $12,000 fine) or can send him or her to jail.

1. Who presides over a trial?
   (A) A judge
   (B) A defendant
   (C) A victim

2. Who decides "guilty" or "innocent"?
   (A) The victim
   (B) The jury
   (C) The judge

3. How many people are usually on a jury?
   (A) Only the judge
   (B) Two
   (C) Twelve

4. Who sentences a criminal?
   (A) The jury
   (B) The prosecutor
   (C) The judge

UNIT ACTIVITIES

START TALKING

1. Job Talk (Class)

Name an occupation. The next student names another occupation, and so forth around the room. The game must be very fast. When a classmate doesn't know an occupation, s/he is "out." The game continues with the next student.

> *Example*
> | | |
> |---|---|
> | Student 1: | Baker |
> | Student 2: | Shoe maker |
> | Student 3: | Teacher |
> | Student 4: | Uhhhhhhh |
> | Everyone: | You're OUT!!! |

Variation 1:
Limit the occupations (indoor or outdoor occupations, jobs in science, jobs in show business, etc.)

Variation 2:
Write down the occupations on a piece of paper or on the board as they are said aloud. At the end of the game, the class can categorize them or alphabetize them. (At the board, two people may be needed to keep up the speed.)

2. Associations (Class)

Name an occupation. The next student will say a word associated with the occupation. Again the game must be fast.

> *Example*
> | | |
> |---|---|
> | Student 1: | teacher |
> | Student 2: | book |
> | | mechanic |
> | Student 3: | car |
> | | pilot |
> | Student 4: | plane |

3. What's my Job (Class)

Think of an occupation. Everyone has to guess your job by asking you Yes/No questions.

> *Example*
> | | |
> |---|---|
> | Student 1: | Do you work in a classroom? |
> | Student 6: | No. |
> | Student 2: | Do you work with wood? |
> | Student 6: | Yes. |
> | Student 3: | Are you a furniture maker? |
> | Student 6: | No. |

Student 4:	Do you build houses?
Student 6:	Yes.
Student 5:	Are you a carpenter?
Student 6:	YES!

4. **Is-There-a-Doctor-in-the-House BINGO?**

Walk around the room and find someone who has had one of these illness or ailments. When you find someone, that person signs his/her name under the illness. The first person to fill a row (or the whole card) wins.

cold	broken bone	cough
earache	sunburn	cavity
the flu	cut finger	appendicitis

Variation:
Make up your own Bingo cards with other illness or ailments.

Put It in Writing

1. Write a note to the school nurse explaining why (you, your child, your sister) was not in school yesterday.

2. Describe the job you have or the job you want.

Variation:
Make the description into a job advertisement. Pass it around the room. If a job is interesting to you, sign your name to it. Then interview for the job with the person who wrote the advertisement. Which jobs are the most interesting?

3. Create an ad for a new beauty product or snack food.

4. Look at the places of business on this street. Complete the store signs with clever names that will attract customers. Compare your names with the names your classmates wrote. Which names are the best? Take a vote for the class favorites.

ACT IT OUT 1

Functions
Describing a profession   Criticizing others
Expressing desire   Expressing fear

Characters
A captain of a boat   A carpenter   A policeman
A teacher   An electrician   A soldier
A doctor   A nurse   A lawyer
An artist   A plumber   A judge
A banker

Setting
A ship is sinking. The captain of a smaller boat can only save two people and take them to safety on a deserted island.

Captain: I can only take two people on my boat.

Doctor: Take me! I'm a doctor. If you get sick, I can cure you. I can give you medicine and injections.

Artist: No, take me! Take me! I'm an artist. If you get bored, I can paint beautiful pictures for you. I can make your life full of color and happiness.

Carpenter:	Take me! I'm a carpenter. If you want a new home, I can build it for you. I can make cabinets and furniture, too.
Electrician:	Yeah, take him and take me! If you want to read at night, I can put electricity in your home. Without me, you can't watch TV!
Plumber:	What about me? If you like to wash your hands, take me! I can put sinks in the kitchen and bathtubs in the bathrooms.
Banker:	All of that will take money. If you want to build a home, you'll need lots of money. Take me! I'm very rich.
Teacher:	Of course, you don't want to be stupid, do you? Of course, not. Be smart and take me! I can teach you everything.
Nurse:	Take me, please! Please, take me. You don't need a doctor. I can take care of you if you are sick.
Lawyer:	Don't you think you will need some legal advice? If you get in trouble, I can get you out of it.
Policeman:	If you take me, there won't be any trouble. I can keep the peace.
Soldier:	I can do it better. Take me if you really want peace.
Judge:	I'm good at making decisions. I'll decide who is the most important. Take me and I'll choose the other important person.
All:	(Desperate) Take me. Please, take me!!!!!!!
Captain:	You must decide yourselves. Write the names of two people who should go with me. Will it be the teacher, the doctor, the artist, the banker, the carpenter, the electrician, the nurse, the plumber, the lawyer, the policeman, the soldier, or the judge? The persons with the most votes will go with me. Write the names now. (The Captain collects the votes and counts them. He announces the group's decision.) The _____ and the _____ will go with me. Bye-bye!

Which two people did the captain take to the deserted island and WHY?

ACT IT OUT 2

Do the skit again. Choose other occupations and tell why they are important.

Warm Up

I'm a _____.
    politician
    student
    janitor
    doorman
    baker
    ...

I can _____.
    lower your taxes
    save the world
    clean your room
    open the door
    bake your bread
    ...

AROUND THE WORLD

How many words from this unit can you identify. Write the words on the lines. Draw lines from the picture to the words.

26 GEOGRAPHY

WORDS TO KNOW

Antarctic Circle	forest	mountain range	sea
Arctic Circle	globe	north	shore
bay	ground	North Pole	south
coast	gulf	ocean	South Pole
continent	hill	peninsula	stream
creek	island	plain	surf
earth	lake	plateau	valley
east	land	pond	waterfall
Equator	map	river	west
field	mountain	river bank	woods

WORD PRACTICE

1. Label the parts of the globe.

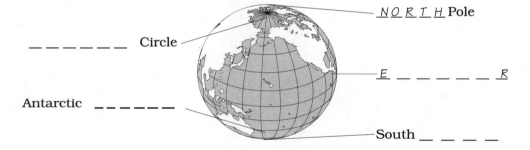

_N O R T H_ Pole

_ _ _ _ _ _ Circle

_E_ _ _ _ _ _ _ _R_

Antarctic _ _ _ _ _ _

South _ _ _ _

2. Circle the correct word.

1. The Sahara and the Mohave are examples of (mountains / deserts).

2. The Nile and Amazon are examples of (oceans / rivers).

3. Everest and Fuji are examples of (mountains / seas).

4. The Atlantic and the Pacific are examples of (continents / oceans).

5. Japan and Hawaii are examples of (islands / peninsulas).

6. Niagara and Victoria are examples of (waterfalls / ponds).

7. The Urals and Andes are examples of (mountain ranges / creeks).

3. Write the geographic term under the appropriate label.

	WATER	LAND
1. ocean	OCEAN	
2. mountain		MOUNTAIN
3. hill		
4. river		
5. shore		
6. pond		
7. valley		
8. creek		
9. stream		
10. peninsula		
11. plateau		
12. sea		
13. surf		
14. continent		
15. lake		
16. bay		

4. Complete the following sentences.

1. A farmer plants wheat in the F I E L D .

2. The flood waters ran over the R __ V __ __ B __ __ __ .

3. Early settlers traveled across the rich fertile P __ __ __ N S .

4. The farm animals drink water from the P __ __ D .

5. Many people work on both the Atlantic and the Pacific
   C __ __ __ T S .

6. The F __ __ __ __ T fires destroyed acres of trees.

7. The E __ __ __ __ is the third planet from the sun.

8. Children learn about the world by studying G __ __ __ __ S and
   M __ __ __ .

5. Complete the directions on the compass.

North

4. _____

West

Northeast

1. _____

3. _____

Southeast

2. _____

READING PRACTICE

1. Which underlined word is incorrect? Circle the letter.

GRAMMAR TO KNOW:	
prepositions	pronouns
subject-verb agreement	verb tense

1. The small stream <u>at</u> the top of the mountain <u>flow</u> into a <u>large</u> river.
                     A   Ⓑ   C

2. The <u>North</u> Pole <u>lie</u> inside <u>the</u> Arctic Circle.
        A   B   C

3. We live <u>on</u> a peninsula, which <u>was</u> a narrow strip <u>of</u> land.
        A   B   C

4. The valley <u>are</u> surrounded by mountains <u>covered</u> <u>with</u> forests.
           A   B   C

5. Tomorrow, Mr. Johnson <u>was</u> flying south of <u>the</u> equator <u>to</u> Rio.
                   A   B   C

6. These fish <u>are</u> too large to live <u>in</u> the lake, so <u>he</u> must live in the ocean.
          A   B   C

7. Look at a map <u>to</u> the bay and <u>count</u> the <u>number</u> of islands.
           A   B   C

8. When the American settlers <u>moved</u> west, <u>it</u> settled <u>on</u> the plains.
                      A   B   C

9. There <u>is</u> a small swimming pond on <u>the</u> other side <u>from</u> that hill.
        A   B   C

10. The forest <u>at</u> the edge of the valley <u>have</u> many kinds <u>of</u> trees.
            A   B   C

2. Read the following conversation and answer the questions.

Man:	Where would you prefer to live? In the mountains or by the sea?
Woman:	I like the dry climate of the desert.
Man:	Not me. I prefer the woods and lakes.
Woman:	There is too much noise in the woods.

1. What does the woman prefer?
   (A) The desert
   (B) The ocean
   (C) The mountains

2. What is characteristic of a desert?
   (A) A dry climate
   (B) A lake
   (C) A sea

3. What does the man prefer?
   (A) The desert
   (B) The woods
   (C) The ocean

4. Where is there too much noise?
   (A) A mountainous island
   (B) An island in a lake
   (C) In the woods

3. Read the following paragraph and answer the questions.

> The Mississippi River begins in the Great Plains. It continues south and empties into the Gulf of Mexico. The Gulf of Mexico borders the eastern coast of Texas and the western shore of Florida. Florida is a peninsula. The Gulf is on its west and the Atlantic Ocean is on its east.

1. Where does the Mississippi River begin?
   (A) In the Great Plains
   (B) At the Gulf of Mexico
   (C) In Texas

2. Which direction does the Mississippi flow?
   (A) North
   (B) East
   (C) South

3. What is Florida?
   (A) A gulf
   (B) A peninsula
   (C) An ocean

4. What is east of Florida?
   (A) The Atlantic Ocean
   (B) The Gulf of Mexico
   (C) Texas

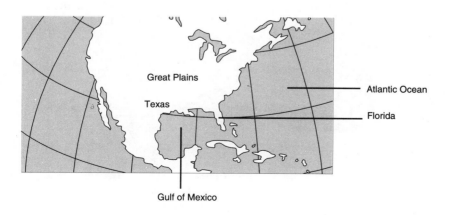

27 THE WEATHER

WORDS TO KNOW

breeze	flood	lightning	sun
clear	forecast	rain	temperature
cloud	freeze	rainstorm	thunder
cold	ground	sky	thunderstorm
cool	hot	snow	warm
drought	humid	snowstorm	wind
dry	ice	storm	windstorm

WORD PRACTICE

1. Draw a line to connect opposites.

warm ———————————— cloudy
dry ————————————— cool
cold   humid
clear   hot

2. Make a compound noun by adding the word *storm* to the following.

rain   *RAINSTORM*_____

thunder   _____

wind   _____

snow   _____

3. Cross out the word that does NOT belong.

1. cool   warm   ~~earth~~   temperature
2. ice   freeze   cold   hot
3. dry   drought   hot   snow
4. wind   breeze   sun   windstorm
5. thunder   lightning   sky   temperature

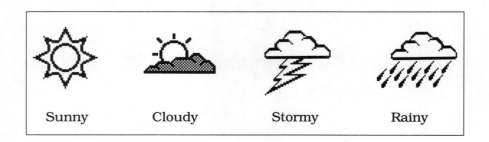

Sunny   Cloudy   Stormy   Rainy

4. Make adjectives out of these words. Add -y.

NOUN	ADJECTIVE
wind	_WINDY_
cloud	_____
snow	_____
storm	_____
rain	_____

> **NOTE THESE DIFFERENCES:**
>
> | NOUN | ADJECTIVE |
> |------|-----------|
> | ice | icy |
> | sun | sunny |
> | breeze | breezy |

5. Complete these sentences with an adjective.

1. There are many <u>clouds</u> in the sky. It's a _CLOUDY_ day.

2. The <u>winds</u> are very strong. It's a _____ day.

3. Five inches of <u>snow</u> will fall. It will be a _____ day.

4. The forecast calls for <u>rainstorms</u>. It will be _____ .

5. The <u>breezes</u> will blow from the south. It will be a _____ morning.

6. The <u>rain</u> will continue until 6 p.m. It will be a _____ day.

7. After the <u>ice</u> storm, the roads will be _____ .

8. The <u>sun</u> will rise at 5:42 a.m., and the day will be _____ .

6. Circle the correct word.

1. The ((sky)/ breeze) is sunny and blue.

2. The noise from the (thunderstorm/cloud) frightened the children.

3. When water (freezes/runs), ice is formed.

4. (Lightning/Snow) during a thunderstorm is caused by electricity.

5. The (temperature/wind) is above 20 degrees Celsius.

6. The (ground/thunder) was wet from the heavy rain.

READING PRACTICE

1. Which underlined word is incorrect? Circle the letter.

> **GRAMMAR TO KNOW:**
> adjectives   articles
> prepositions   subject-verb agreement

1. Tomorrow <u>the</u> weather will <u>be</u> hot and <u>humidity</u>.
          A   B   Ⓒ

2. <u>The</u> roads <u>was</u> <u>icy</u> after the storm.
     A   B C

3. <u>There</u> were few <u>clouds</u> <u>on</u> the sky.
     A   B   C

4. The <u>temperature</u> today <u>is</u> as <u>higher</u> as yesterday.
         A   B   C

5. <u>The</u> thunder <u>usually</u> <u>follows</u> lightning.
     A   B   C

6. <u>There</u> <u>were</u> a <u>cool</u>, pleasant breeze this afternoon.
     A   B   C

7. The earth's temperature <u>are</u> raised <u>by</u> the heat <u>of</u> the sun.
                     A   B   C

8. <u>The</u> thunderstorms <u>are</u> caused by warm air <u>meeting</u> cold air.
     A   B   C

9. Yesterday's snowstorm <u>put</u> four inches <u>in</u> snow <u>on</u> the ground.
                  A   B   C

10. In January, the temperature often <u>goes</u> below freezing and the sky is often
                                 A

    <u>covered</u> with <u>the</u> clouds.
     B   C

RAIN EXPRESSIONS

The following expressions mean
"It's raining a lot":

1. It's raining cats and dogs.

2. It's coming down in buckets.

3. It's pouring.

4. It's raining really hard.

2. Read the following paragraph and answer the following questions.

> The lack of rain in the Southwest is causing a drought. However, in the Northeast rainstorms are causing floods. In the Northwest, the weather is normal.

1. Where is there no rain?
   (A) In the Northeast
   (B) In the Southwest
   (C) In the Northwest

2. What causes a drought?
   (A) Lack of rain
   (B) Rainstorms
   (C) Farmers

3. What causes floods?
   (A) Lack of rain
   (B) Rainstorms
   (C) Droughts

4. Where are there floods?
   (A) In the Northeast
   (B) In the Southwest
   (C) In the Northwest

3. Read the following weather report and answer the questions.

> This afternoon the weather will be hot and humid with the temperature above 40 degrees Celsius. This evening we will have thunderstorms with the possibility of 2-3 inches of rain. By morning the sky will be clear and tomorrow's weather will be sunny and breezy.

1. What is this afternoon's weather?
   (A) Hot and humid
   (B) Cool and dry
   (C) Warm and breezy

2. When will the thunderstorms begin?
   (A) Sometime this afternoon
   (B) In the evening
   (C) Tomorrow morning

3. How much rain is predicted?
   (A) 40 inches
   (B) 23 inches
   (C) 2-3 inches

4. What is tomorrow's forecast?
   (A) Cold and breezy
   (B) Sunny and humid
   (C) Clear and sunny

UNIT ACTIVITIES

START TALKING

1. **Name that Capital (Class Game)**

Name a country. The next student names its capital. When a student doesn't know the capital, s/he is "out." The game continues with the next student.

Example
Student 1:   Morocco
Student 2:   Rabat
                           Norway
Student 3:   Oslo
                           Canada
Student 4:   Vancouver

Everyone: !!!! WRONG!!!! You're OUT!

2. **Earth or Water (Class Game)**

Think of a geographical feature (a mountain, a river, a lake). The other students ask Yes/No questions to guess it.

Example
Student 1:   Is it made of water?
Student 2:   Yes.
Student 3:   Is it a river?
Student 2:   No.
Student 4:   Is it larger than a lake?
Student 2:   Yes.
Student 5:   Is it in the Eastern Hemisphere?
Student 2:   No.
Student 6:   Is it in the Northern Hemisphere?
Student 2:   Yes.
Student 7:   Is it the Gulf of Mexico?
Student 2:   YES!

3. **Touring (Class Game)**

Name a famous historical tourist attraction. The next student tells where it is. When a student doesn't know the location, s/he is "out." The game starts over.

Example
Student 1:   I'm looking at the Eifel Tower.
Student 2:   You must be in Paris.
                           I'm looking at the Great Wall.
Student 3:   You must be in China.

4. Hangman (Class or Partners)

Think of a country, capital, or geographical feature. On a piece of paper (or on the board with the whole class) put a dash for each letter of the word or phrase. The other student(s) guess the letters and try to guess the word. For each incorrect guess, draw a body part. Try to guess the word before the man is "hanged." Hint: Guess the vowels first!

Incorrect Guesses
i u w b l

(Grand Canyon) _ _ a _ _ _ a _ _ o _

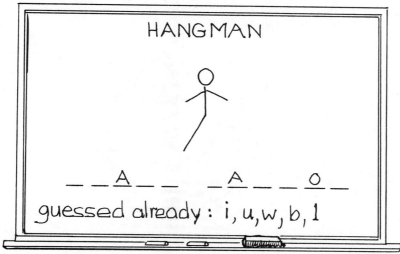

5. Border Guards (Class or Partners)

Describe a country's location. Your classmate will guess the country.

Student 1: This country is bordered on the north by Canada, on the south by Mexico, on the west by the Pacific Ocean, and on the east by the Atlantic Ocean.

Student 2: Is it Peru?
Student 1: NO!! You're OUT!

PUT IT IN WRITING

1. Choose a place in the world you want to visit. Write a description of the place.

   Pass your description to other students. If they like the description and want to go there, they will sign their name under your description. How many people want to come with you?

2. Describe your favorite season. Tell why you like it.

   Variation:
   Describe your least favorite season. Tell why you hate it.

ACT IT OUT 1

Functions

Giving orders
Expressing confusion
Expressing excitement
Expressing annoyance
Giving explanations
Describing weather

Characters

Mission Control
Astronaut 1
Astronaut 2
Astronaut 3

Setting

Three astronauts are in a space shuttle orbiting the earth. They receive their orders from Mission Control on the Earth.

Mission Control:	Good morning, Astronauts!
Astronaut 1:	(Sleepy) What? Who? Where?
Mission Control:	Good morning! Wake up! It's time to work!
Astronaut 1:	(Unhappy) Call back in an hour. We're sleeping.
Mission Control:	(Angry) Wake up! Get to work.
Astronaut 2:	Now what?
Mission Control:	Look out your windows. What do you see?
Astronaut 1:	Stars.
Astronaut 2:	Me, too. I see stars.
Astronaut 3:	Yeah. Stars.
Mission Control:	Look down! Look down! What do you see?
Astronaut 1:	Oh, yeah. The Earth.
Astronaut 2:	Yeah, I see it.
Astronaut 3:	Me, too. I see the Earth.
Mission Control:	(Sarcastic) Good! Now get out your camera.
Astronaut 1:	Who has the camera?
Astronaut 2:	Not me.
Astronaut 3:	I do. I do.
Mission Control:	OK. Now take some pictures. You're over California. You're going west.
Astronaut 2:	(Excited) We're over the Pacific Ocean now. Take a picture of

	Hawaii.
Astronaut 1:	(More excited) Too late. We're over Japan now. Take a picture of Tokyo.
Astronaut 3:	I can't see it. It's too cloudy there.
Astronaut 2:	(Even more excited) We're over China now. Take a picture of the Great Wall.
Astronaut 1:	(More excited) Too late. We're over the Himalayas now. Take a picture of Mt. Everest.
Astronaut 3:	I can't see it. It's snowing there.
Astronaut 2:	(Still more excited) We're over Turkey now. Take a picture of Ankara.
Astronaut 1:	(Very, very excited) Too late. We're over Europe now. Take a picture of Italy.
Astronaut 3:	I can't see it. It's raining there.
Mission Control:	What can you see? Take a picture of something!
Astronaut 3:	Uh Oh! I can't.
Mission Control:	Why not?
Astronaut 3:	We forgot the film.

ACT IT OUT 2

Mission Control is asking you to take more pictures on another trip. Pick a location as a starting point and repeat the dialogue for the new orbit. Hint: You can orbit around the middle of the Earth around the equator. Or, you can orbit from top to bottom from the North Pole to the South Pole.

Warm Up

We're over _____. Take a picture of _____

hemisphere	
continent	continent
country	country
ocean	capital
region	island
	geographical feature

I can't see it. It's (bad weather condition) there.
    rainy
    cloudy
    snowy
    stormy

Words Used by Real People

Yeah
Yeah is an everyday way to say *yes*. Good friends will say it to one another. it is rarely used when talking to someone respected (like your employer, parents, or teacher). Here the astronaut uses Yeah because he is talking to his close friends.

Uh Oh
This sound means there is a problem or you made a mistake. Uh oh.

ANSWER KEY

AT HOME

1 BODY

Word Practice

1. Right Side
   head
   neck
   chest
   arm
   hand
   knee
   ankle
   Left Side
   nose
   wrist
   elbow
   waist
   hip
   leg
   foot
2. 2. elbow
   3. palm; hand
   4. leg
   5. feet
   6. muscle
   7. lips
   8. shoulder
   9. stomach
   10. thumbs
   11. mouth
   12. tongue
   13. eyes
   14. cheek
   15. hand
   16. heart
   17. heart
   18. neck
   19. eye; eye
   20. back
3. 2. nose
   3. chin
   4. nails
   5. forehead
4. 2. thigh
   3. neck
   4. ankle
   5. eye
   6. wrist
   7. forehead
   8. throat
   9. head
   10. nail

Reading Practice

1. 1. B hurt
   2. A close
   3. B pumps
   4. C walking
   5. B has
   6. C the
   7. B are
   8. A eating
   9. C see
   10. C no article
2. 1. C   3. 1. B
   2. A   2. B
   3. B   3. C
   4. C   4. A

2 CLOTHES

Word Practice

1. 2. raincoat; umbrella
   3. shoelace
   4. belt
   5. sweater
   6. collar
   7. button
   8. skirt; handbag
   9. jacket
   10. cuffs
2. raincoat - overcoat
   tennis shoes -
     sneakers
   pants - slacks
3. 2. jacket

---

3. cuff
4. skirt
5. shoe
6. collar
7. suit/jacket
8. tie
9. shirt
10. pants
4. 2. slacks
   3. shoes
   4. gloves
   5. trousers
   6. socks
   7. boots
5. Worn above
   shirt
   T-shirt
   sweater
   jacket
   Worn below
   boots
   shorts
   running shoes
   shoe laces
   tennis shoes
6. 1. on, put
   2. off, take
   3. away
7. 2. hat
   3. scarf; tie

Reading Practice

1. 1. B to be
   2. B and
   3. A get
   4. C is
   5. A wears
   6. A am
   7. C and
   8. B doesn't
   9. C are
   10. A to wear
2. 1. A   3. 1. B
   2. B   2. A
   3. C   3. C
   4. C   4. A

3 LIVING ROOM

Word Practice

1. 2. woodwork
   3. mantel
   4. picture
   5. shelves
   6. painting
2. 2. shelves
   3. end tables
   4. drapes
   5. pictures
   6. chairs
3. 2. in
   3. to
   4. above
   5. under
   6. on
4. mantel
   shelf
   mirror
   painting
5. 2. of
   3. in front of
   4. behind
   5. across from
   6. in
   7. between
   8. beside
   9. next to
   10. in front of
6. 2. woodwork
   3. ashtray
   4. armchair
   5. bookcase
   6. fireplace

Reading Practice

1. 1. A in
   2. C is
   3. B and
   4. B has

---

5. A on/over
6. A and
7. C matches
8. B are
9. C appears
10. B allow
2. 1. A   3. 1. B
   2. B   2. C
   3. C   3. A
   4. C   4. C

4 KITCHEN

Word Practice

1. 2. toaster
   3. refrigerator
   4. coffee maker
   5. garbage disposal
2. glass
   spoon
   salt shaker
   cup
   napkin
3. 2. saucer
   3. sink
   4. cabinet
   5. tablecloth
   6. garbage
   7. placemat
   8. bowl
   9. broiler
   10. cup
4. 2. knife
   3. glass
   4. stove
   5. salt shaker
   6. dish
   7. bottle
   8. cabinet
   9. placemat
   10. napkin
5. 2. plant
   3. lamp
   4. ceiling
   5. seat
   6. window
6. 2. fork
   3. pans
   4. pepper
7. 2. coffee maker
   3. garbage disposal
   4. oven
   5. toaster

Reading Practice

1. 1. C and
   2. B and
   3. A have
   4. A her
   5. C no article
   6. A has
   7. A We
   8. C it
   9. B was
   10. C or
2. 1. C   3. 1. C
   2. B   2. B
   3. A   3. B
   4. C   4. C

5 HOUSEWORK

Word Practice

1. 2. dusting
   3. washing
   4. cleaning
   5. polishing
   6. ironing
   7. drying
2. 2. cleaning
   3. washing
   4. dusting
   5. Polishing
   6. ironing
   7. scrubbing
   8. mopping
3. sponge - rag

---

soap - cleanser
wash - clean
sweep - vacuum
4. 2. cord
   3. sweep
   4. shower
   5. yard
5. 2. cleanser
   3. rug shampoo
   4. polish
   5. detergent
   6. ammonia
   7. bleach
   8. soap
6. 2. Bleach
   3. cleanser
   4. detergent
   5. polish
   6. paper towels
   7. water
   8. rug shampoo

Reading Practice

1. 1. A To sweep
   2. B and
   3. C try
   4. A was
   5. B scrubs
   6. C and
   7. A will
   8. A Pour
   9. C makes
   10. A clean
2. 1. A   3. 1. A
   2. A   2. C
   3. C   3. B
   4. A   4. B

6 FOOD

Word Practice

1. Dairy Goods
   2. eggs
   3. cheese
   4. milk
   5. cream
   Baked Goods
   1. crackers
   2. cake
   3. cookies
   4. bread
   5. pie
2. 2. fish
   3. milk
   4. drive
   5. animal
3. bread - butter
   coffee - cream
   salt - pepper
   ice cream - cake
   tomatoes -
     lettuce
   oil - vinegar
4. 2. fish
   3. corn
   4. rice
   5. lettuce
   6. sugar
   7. cheese
   8. bacon
   9. milk
   10. pepper
5. 2. potatoes
   3. grapes
   4. beans
   5. onions
   6. cookies
6. 1. eggs
   flour
   milk
   sugar
   2. lettuce
   oil
   vinegar
   tomatoes
   3. bread
   butter
   lettuce
   chicken

tomatoes
4. meat
   salt
   pepper
   carrots
   onions

Reading Practice
1. 1. B found
   2. A is
   3. C for
   4. C and
   5. C for
   6. A is
   7. B take
   8. A make
   9. C in
   10. C on
2. 1. A   3. 1. B
   2. C   2. C
   3. B   3. A
   4. A   4. B

7 MONEY

Word Practice
1.   coins - change
     wallet - billfold
     money plan -
        budget
     cash - money
     dime - ten cents
     credit card - charge
        card
     one cent - penny
2. 2. charge
   3. pay
   4. earn
   5. save
3. 2. tax
   3. forget
   4. meal
   5. pen
4. 1. quarter; dime
   2. dimes; nickel
   3. quarters
   4. nickels; dimes
   5. quarters; pennies;
        dollar
5. 2. check
   3. receipt
   4. piggybank
   5. taxes
   6. credit card
6. 2. credit card
   3. billfold
   4. payment
   5. budget

Reading Practice
1. 1. A keeps
   2. A would
   3. C have
   4. C to/on
   5. B in
   6. A a
   7. A have
   8. C should
   9. A The
   10. C to
2. 1. B   3. 1. B
   2. A   2. A
   3. B   3. C
   4. A   4. B

ACROSS
THE CITY

8 THE CITY

Word Practice
1. 2. street light
   3. stop sign
   4. street sign
   5. subway station
   6. bus stop
   7. telephone booth
   8. newspaper stand
2. 2. city hall
   3. movie theater
   4. apartment house
   5. concert hall

6. museum
7. opera house
8. hospital
9. hotel
3. 1. street
   2. road
   3. highway
   4. alley
   5. freeway
   6. lane
   7. drive
   8. boulevard
4.   sidewalk
     curb
     crosswalk
5.   parking meter
     parking lot

Reading Practice
1. 1. B on
   2. C had turned
   3. B and
   4. B parking
   5. C going
   6. B to
   7. C stay
   8. A on
   9. A Get
   10. C and
2. 1. A   3. 1. A
   2. B   2. C
   3. B   3. A
   4. A   4. B

9 BANKS

Word Practice
1.   <u>People</u>
     bank manager
     customer
     <u>Money</u>
     interest
     service charge
     cash
     balance
     <u>Form</u>
     bank slip
     deposit slip
     withdrawal slip
2. 2. lending
   3. cashing
   4. Withdrawing
   5. Borrowed
   6. ATM
3. 1. 2
   2. $642.00
   3. $904.67
   4. $ 6.42
   5. $ 40.00
4.   withdrawal
     teller
     teller's window
     balance
     transaction
5. 2. District Loan Co.
   3. Oct 5, 1991
   4. $55.00
   5. car loan payment
   6. 546
6.   teller - customer
     deposit - withdrawal
     interest-service charge
     lend - borrow
7. 2. lending
   3. withdrawing
   4. checking
   5. banking
   6. borrowing

Reading Practice
1. 1. C fill
   2. C cashing
   3. A to make
   4. B of
   5. B lend
   6. C on
   7. C to inquire
   8. B for
   9. A to balance
   10. A driving
2. 1. C   3. 1. B
   2. A   2. C
   3. B   3. B
   4. C   4. C

10 RESTAURANTS

Word Practice
1. 2. reservation
   3. bartender
   4. lunch
   5. service
2. 1. breakfast
   2. lunch
   3. afternoon snack
   4. dinner
3. 2. high
   3. slow
   4. dirty
   5. smoky
4. 2. napkin
   3. glass
   4. spoon
   5. plate
   6. fork
   7. knife
   8. placemat
5. 2. soft drink
   3. waitress
   4. smoking section
   5. snack
   6. check
   7. tip
   8. silverware
6. 2. always
   3. sometimes
   4. never
   5. sometimes

Reading Practice
1. 1. A would
   2. C and
   3. A Put
   4. B she
   5. B will
   6. B have
   7. C and
   8. A You
   9. C their
   10. A is
2. 1. C   3. 1. B
   2. B   2. B
   3. C   3. C
   4. A   4. B

11 ENTERTAINMENT

Word Practice
1. 2. director
   3. actor / actress
   4. performer
   5. singer
2. 2. television
   3. laughter
   4. music
   5. sit
3.   symphony
     opera
     play
     musical
     movie
     comedy
4.   symphony
     opera
     musical
     rock
5. 2. film-movie
   3. symphony-concert
   4. drama-play
   5. director-conductor
   6. star-actress
6.   <u>Person</u>
     audience
     cast
     chorus
     musician
     <u>Action</u>
     conduct
     direct
     perform
     <u>Location</u>
     box
     cinema
7. 2. cast
   3. chorus
   4. row
   5. playhouse

Reading Practice
1. 1. B get
   2. B or
   3. B listening
   4. C in
   5. A performing
   6. B of
   7. B to please
   8. B to eat
   9. A to use
   10. B for
2. 1. B   3. 1. B
   2. A   2. A
   3. C   3. B
   4. A   4. C

12 POST OFFICE

Word Practice
1. 2. letter
   3. stamp
   4. clerk; counter
   5. postmark
   6. parcel
   7. office box
   8. zip code
   9. label
   10. first class
2.   postal clerk
     postal code
     postcard
     post mark
     post office box
3. 2. I see my mail.
   3. I open the envelope.
   4. I read the letter.
   5. I write a reply.
   6. I put my reply into
        an envelope.
   7. I seal and stamp my
        letter.
   8. I take it to the post
        office.
4. 2. weigh
   3. post office
   4. surface
   5. postmark
5. 2. address
   3. postmark
   4. stamp

Reading Practice
1. 1. B add
   2. C in
   3. B on
   4. B sold
   5. C was
   6. B sort
   7. A postmark
   8. A mail
   9. A was
   10. B label
2. 1. C   3. 1. C
   2. B   2. A
   3. A   3. C
   4. B   4. B

13 GAS STATION

Word Practice
1. 1. hood
   2. tires; air
   3. windshield
   4. gas tank; fill it up
   5. trunk
2. 2. paper
   3. rain
   4. take a break
   5. oil
3.   service station -
        gas station
     gas - fuel
     repair - fix a problem
     mechanic - car
        repairman
4.   oil
     grease
     air
5. 2. change
   3. check
   4. pump
   5. repair
6. 2. changing
   3. check

4. pumps
5. repairing
7. 2. oil
3. change
4. hood
5. trunk
8. 2. hood
3. tire
4. trunk

Reading Practice
1. 1. B should/must
2. C to fill
3. C to change
4. A checks the oil in her car once a week.
5. A walks
6. B should
7. B to see
8. A is
9. A is
10. B need to be replaced once a year.
2. 1. A   3. 1. B
2. A   2. C
3. B   3. B

ON THE ROAD

14 HOTEL

Word Practice
1. 2. register; check in
3. check out
4. tip; luggage
2. front desk
check out
room service
double bed
3. 2. desk clerk
3. check out
4. double bed
5. room service
4. 2. bellman
3. doorman
4. maid
5. elevators
6. lobby
7. tip
8. room service
5. checked in
clerk
front desk
registered
key
bellman
luggage
suite
6. Person
doorman
elevator operator
guest
maid
Action
register
reserve
Location
floor
front desk
lobby
room
suite
7. 1. 2   5. 5
2. 3   6. 8
3. 1   7. 6
4. 4   8. 7

Reading Practice
1. 1. C asked
2. B don't
3. A would
4. B need
5. A and
6. B while
7. B in
8. C and
9. B and
10. B ask
2. 1. A   3. 1. C
2. C   2. B
3. B   3. A
4. C   4. B

15 PLANES

Word Practice
1. 2. departure
3. dining
4. arrival
5. reservation
6. smoking
7. driver
2. on time - late
deplane-board
smoking-non smoking
take off - land
round trip-one way
economy class - first class
3. 2. passport
3. overhead
4. runway
5. customs
4. 2. lawyer
3. station
4. dining car
5. coins
6. luggage
5. Person
flight attendant
passenger
pilot
ticket agent
reservation clerk
Place
airport
coach
control tower
economy class
gate
overhead bin
plane
runway
6. 2. air traffic controller
3. reservation clerk/ travel agent
4. pilot
5. steward/ stewardess/ flight attendant

Reading Practice
1. 1. B go
2. B to buy
3. B is
4. B stow
5. A have
6. C at
7. A inform
8. A smoke
9. C cancelled
10. B need
2. 1. B   3. 1. A
2. B   2. A
3. A   3. C
4. C   4. B

16 TRAINS

Word Practice
1. 2. conductor
3. passengers
4. timetable
5. track
2. ticket
conductor
ticket
snack bar
dining car
3. 2. travel
3. reserve
4. arrive
5. board
4. Person
engineer
passenger
Action
board
depart
reserve
Thing
ticket
timetable
5. 2. express
3. reserved
4. snack bar

5. luggage rack; seat
6. 2. fare
3. schedule/timetable
4. board
5. gate
6. seat
7. 2. departs
3. reservation
4. board

Reading Practice
1. 1. C eat
2. A is
3. C but
4. C in
5. A stay
6. B and
7. A Look
8. C depart
9. C in
10. C call
2. 1. C   3. 1. B
2. B   2. C
3. B   3. B
4. A   4. A

17 CARS

Word Practice
1. 2. windshield wipers
3. tires
4. wheels
5. bumpers
6. taillights
2. dashboard
windshield
headlights
3. 2. brakes
3. wheels
4. seat belts
5. seats
6. headlights
7. windshield wipers
8. taillights
9. tires
10. turn signals
4. 2. bumper
3. wiper
4. accelerator
5. radiator
5. steering wheel
windshield wiper
passenger seat
glove compartment
turn signal
rearview mirror
gas tank
license plate
seat belt
6. Glove Compartment
extra change
pencil
Trunk
spare tire
jack

Reading Practice
1. 1. A careful
2. C would
3. C comfortable
4. A fill
5. C would
6. B wear
7. A on
8. B conveniently
9. B test
10. A on
2. 1. A   3. 1. A
2. A   2. B
3. B   3. B
4. C   4. C

18 ROADS

Word Practice
1. 2. throughway
3. beltway
4. freeway
5. highway
2. 2. pass
3. drive

4. yield
5. speed
6. honk
3. speed
highway
pass
signal
4. Vehicle
trailer
truck
motorcycle
bus
Action
merge
honk
yield
drive (v.)
Location
highway
overpass
lane
median
rest stop
drive (n.)
5. toll
turnpikes
booths
exits
6. 2. motorbike
3. trailer
4. truck
5. van
7. 2. motorbike
3. overpass
4. motorcycle
5. turnpike

Reading Practice
1. 1. B to get
2. C to
3. A don't
4. B but
5. C pull
6. A on
7. B and
8. A pay
9. B to drive
10. B merge
2. 1. B   3. 1. A
2. A   2. B
3. B   3. B
4. C   4. A

IN BUSINESS

19 TYPES/B'NESS

Word Practice
1. 2. bananas
3. shoes
4. lumber
5. motor oil
6. boats
7. cushions
8. stationery
9. computers
10. rubber band
2. 2. jeweler
3. hair stylist
4. grocer
5. pharmacist
3. 2. luggage store
3. department store
4. drug store
5. record store
4. 2. Yes, you can. At the toy store between the furniture store and the shoe store.
3. Yes, you can. At the hair salon between the drug store and the candy store.
4. Yes, you can. At the bike shop between the art gallery and the drug store.
5. Yes, you can. At the furniture store between the dress

shop and the toy store.
5. 2. compact discs
   3. chocolate bars
   4. racing bikes
   5. prescr. medicine
   6. sandals
   7. overnight bags

Reading Practice

1. 1. B opening
   2. B to
   3. C is
   4. B at
   5. A shopping
   6. C no article
   7. C go
   8. A no article
   9. C attract
   10. C to
2. 1. C   3. 1. C
   2. C   2. C
   3. A   3. A
   4. C   4. A

20 OFFICE TERMS

Word Practice

1. 2. out-box
   3. file cabinet
   4. envelope
   5. outside line
   6. desk
   7. clerical
   8. manager
2. file - file cabinet
   mistake - correction
   envelope - letter
   drawer - desk
   in box-out box
3. 2. client
   3. pen
   4. calendar
   5. telephone
4. paper clip
   paper
   pen
   pencil
5. telephone
   messages
   boss
6. clip-attach
   file cabinet-file
   envelope-mail
   wastebasket-throw
      away
7. 2. paper clip
   3. in basket
   4. out basket

Reading Practice

1. 1. A on
   2. B uses
   3. A have
   4. C answer
   5. B in
   6. B and
   7. A ordered
   8. C in
   9. C start
   10. B give
2. 1. B   3. 1. B
   2. A   2. B
   3. B   3. C
   4. C   4. B

21 OFFICE EQUIP.

Word Practice

1. 2. operator
   3. typewriter
   4. photocopier
   5. stapler
   6. calculator
2. 2. calculator
   3. computer
   4. stapler
   5. photocopier
   6. word processor
   7. voicemail
3. Machines
   answering machine
   computer

telephone
word processor
photocopier
People
secretary
typist
employee
client
4. facsimile - fax
   photocopy - copy
   memorandum - memo
   telephone - phone
5. Types
   memorandum
   fax
   letter
   Ways to Prepare
   word processor
   electric typewriter
   by hand
   Ways to Send
   fax
   by hand/courier
6. 2. pencil
   3. photocopy
   4. drawer
   5. mistakes

Reading Practice

1. 1. A store
   2. A became
   3. C to send
   4. A makes
   5. C on
   6. A answers
   7. C from/to
   8. A in
   9. B uses
   10. C to return
2. 1. B   3. 1. B
   2. B   2. C
   3. A   3. C
   4. A   4. A

22 CONSTRUCTION

Word Practice

1. to measure - ruler
   to cut - saw
   to drain - sink
   to screw - screwdriver
   to sand - sandpaper
   to turn on - power
2. toolbox
   saw
   hammer
   drill
   file
   nails
   screws
   ruler
   measure
   wood
   cuts
3. 2. hammering
   3. drilling
   4. sanding
   5. draining
   6. leaking
   7. dripping
   8. plugging
   9. turning on
   10. looking for
4. 2. leak
   3. fuse
   4. screwdriver
   5. sink
   6. measure
   7. work bench
   8. window
   9. wire
   10. saw
5. sandpaper
   toolbox
   workbench
   screwdriver
6. sink
   drain
   plumber
   plunger
   pipes

Reading Practice

1. 1. B on
   2. B used
   3. A working
   4. B with
   5. B does
   6. A letting
   7. A come
   8. C turn
   9. B fixed
   10. B in
2. 1. B   3. 1. A
   2. B   2. C
   3. C   3. B
   4. B   3. C

423 MEDICINE

Word Practice

1. hurt - ache
   medication - medicine
   physician - doctor
   sick - ill
   illness - disease
2. 2. dentist
   3. patients
   4. broken
   5. prescription
3. 2. medication
   3. operation
   4. injury
   5. treatment
   6. infection
4. Doctors
   x ray
   broken
   headache
   infection
   Dentists
   x ray
   broken
   tooth
   toothache
   infection
5. 2. operation
   3. cold
   4. ambulance
   5. broken
   6. x ray
   7. bone
6. hospital
   nurse
   medication
   pills
   injections
   x ray
   operation
   doctor
7. Person
   nurse
   patient
   Condition
   fever
   headache
   infection
   sore
   Thing
   bandage
   medicine
   drill

Reading Practice

1. 1. B and
   2. C to take
   3. B for
   4. B to save
   5. A removed
   6. C gave
   7. A and
   8. B to
   9. A stay
   10. C in
2. 1. B   3. 1. C
   2. A   2. A
   3. C   3. B
   4. A   4. C

24 MILITARY

Word Practice

1. 2. barracks
   3. submarine
   4. uniform

5. troops
6. drill
2. 2. duty
   3. uniform
   4. base
   5. combat
3. 2. drilling
   3. enlisting
   4. inspecting
   5. sailing
   6. marching
   7. recruiting
   8. joining
4. drill - practice
   base - "town"
   uniform - clothes
   combat - fighting
   barracks -
      dormitory
5. Persons
   soldier
   officer
   Transportation
   tank
   Place
   camp
   barracks

Reading Practice

1. 1. B into
   2. C on
   3. C would
   4. B and
   5. A and
   6. C and
   7. B hopes
   8. B be
   9. C enlist
   10. A practices
2. 1. B   3. 1. C
   2. B   2. B
   3. A   3. A
   4. A   4. B

25 POLICE/LAW

Word Practice

1. violation -
      misdemeanor
   jail - prison
   patrol car -
      police car
   thief - robber
   attorney - lawyer
2. 2. criminal
   3. prosecutor
   4. judge
   5. thief
   6. prisoner
3. 2. sentenced
   3. booked
   4. arrested
   5. imprisoned
   6. judged
   7. witnessed
4. 2. witnesses
   3. judges
   4. sentences
   5. arrests
5. 2. testimony
   3. violation/violator
   4. imprisonment
   5. prosecution/
      prosecutor
   6. defense/defender
   7. robbery/robber

Reading Practice

1. 1. B with
   2. C worst
   3. A have
   4. C to testify
   5. B brought from/
      brought out of
   6. B to wear
   7. C the longest
   8. B to grab
   9. C look for
   10. A will
2. 1. A   3. 1. A
   2. C   2. B
   3. B   3. C
   4. B   4. C

Around the World

26 Geography

Word Practice

1. Arctic Circle
   Equator
   Antarctic Circle
   South Pole
2. 2. rivers
   3. mountains
   4. oceans
   5. islands
   6. waterfalls
   7. mountain ranges
3. Water
   river
   pond
   creek
   stream
   sea
   surf
   lake
   bay
   Land
   hill
   shore
   valley
   peninsula
   plateau
   continent
4. 2. river bank
   3. plains
   4. pond
   5. coasts
   6. forest
   7. earth
   8. globes; maps
5. 1. East
   2. South
   3. Southwest
   4. Northwest

Reading Practice

1. 1. B flows
   2. B lies
   3. B is
   4. A is
   5. A is
   6. C they
   7. A of
   8. B they
   9. C of
   10. B has
2. 1. A
   2. A
   3. B
   4. C
3. 1. A
   2. C
   3. B
   4. A

27 Weather

Word Practice

1. dry - humid
   cold - hot
   clear - cloudy
2. thunderstorm
   windstorm
   snowstorm
3. 2. hot
   3. snow
   4. sun
   5. temperature
4. cloudy
   snowy
   stormy
   rainy
5. 2. windy
   3. snowy
   4. stormy/rainy
   5. breezy
   6. rainy
   7. icy
   8. sunny
6. 2. thunderstorm
   3. freezes
   4. Lightning
   5. temperature
   6. ground

Reading Practice

1. 1. C humid
   2. B were
   3. C in
   4. C high
   5. A no article
   6. B was
   7. A is
   8. A no article
   9. B of
   10. C no article
2. 1. B
   2. A
   3. B
   4. A
3. 1. A
   2. B
   3. C
   4. C